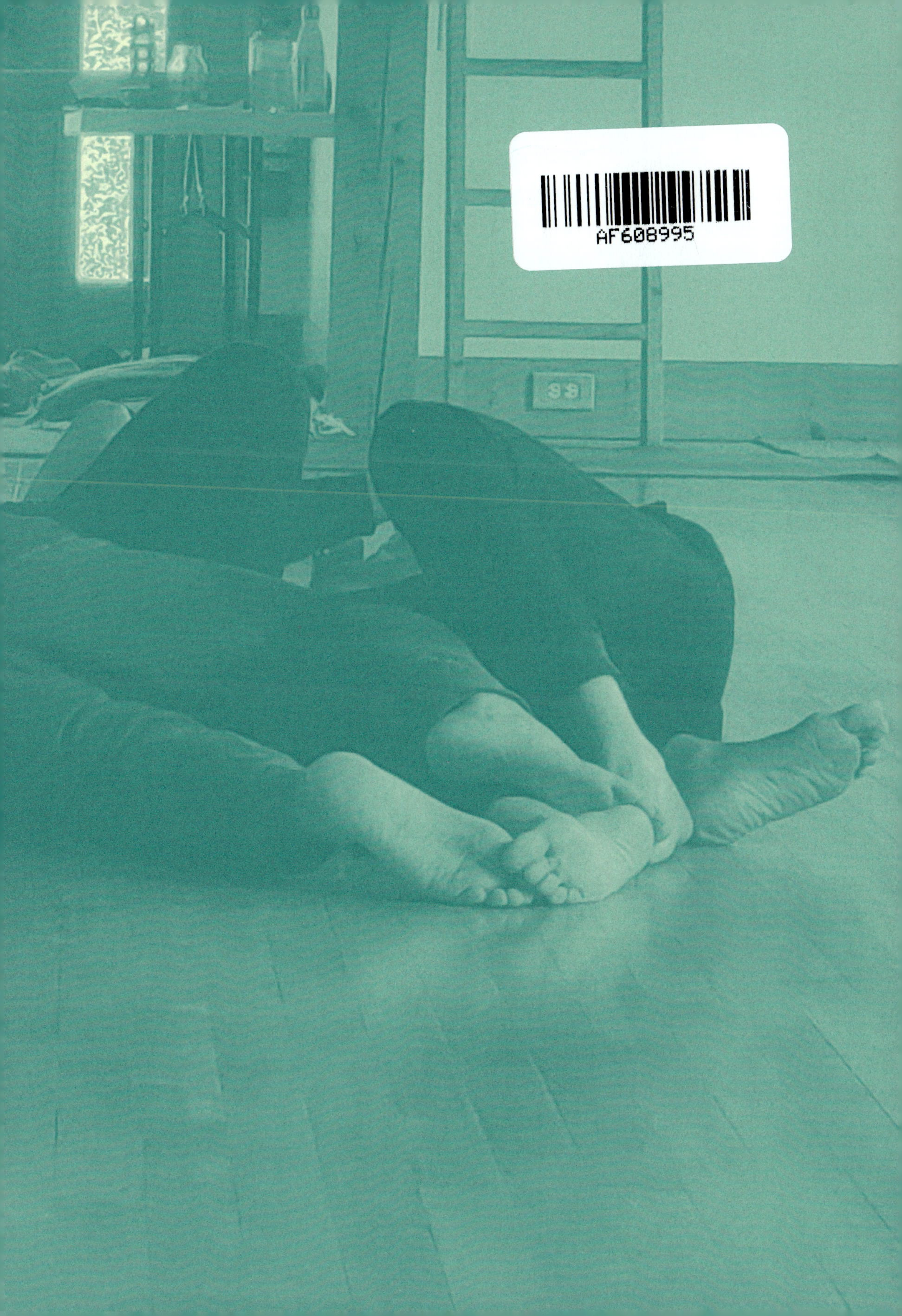

duets

OTHER WAYS OF "WRITING"

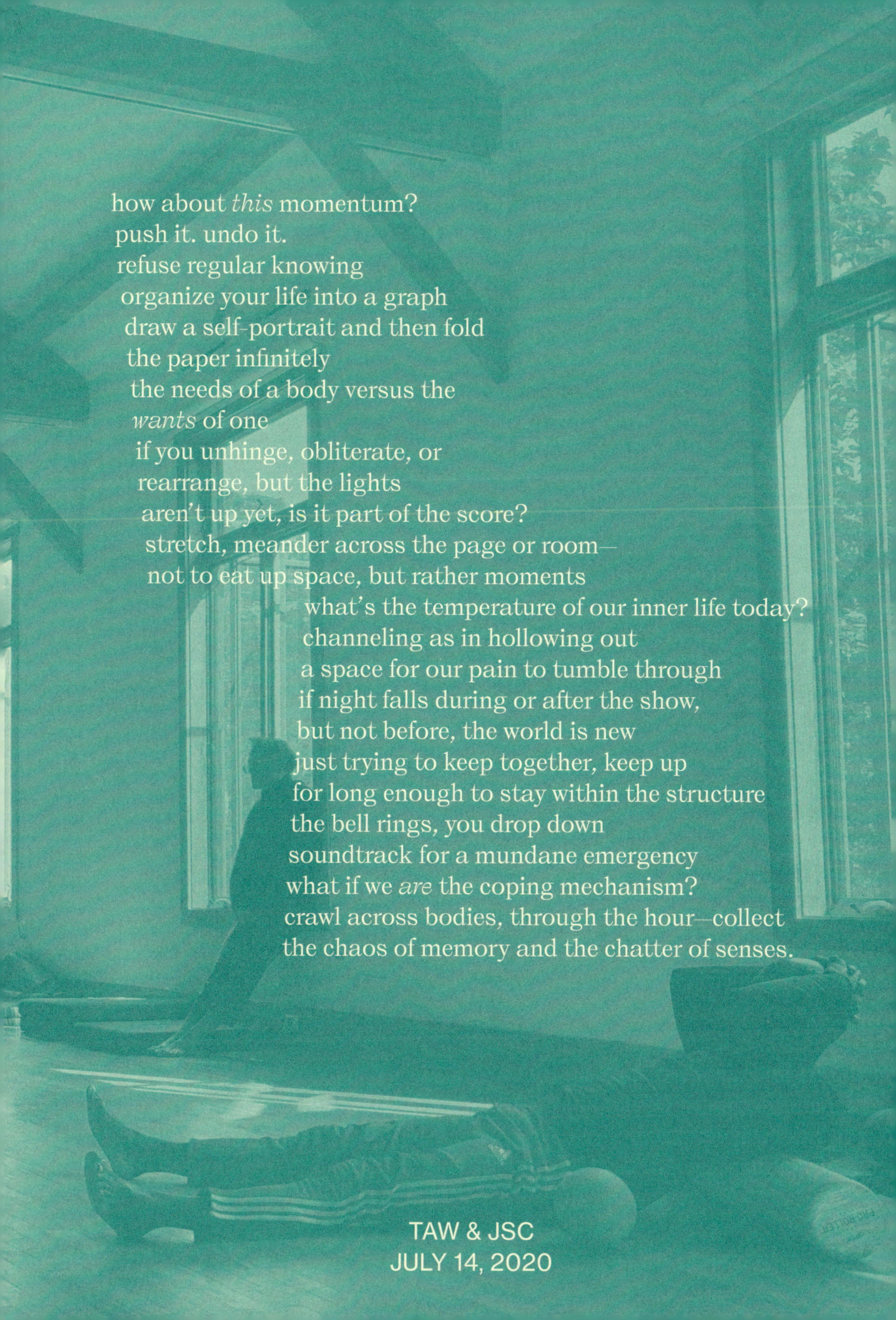

how about *this* momentum?
push it. undo it.
refuse regular knowing
organize your life into a graph
draw a self-portrait and then fold
the paper infinitely
the needs of a body versus the
wants of one
if you unhinge, obliterate, or
rearrange, but the lights
aren't up yet, is it part of the score?
stretch, meander across the page or room—
not to eat up space, but rather moments
what's the temperature of our inner life today?
channeling as in hollowing out
a space for our pain to tumble through
if night falls during or after the show,
but not before, the world is new
just trying to keep together, keep up
for long enough to stay within the structure
the bell rings, you drop down
soundtrack for a mundane emergency
what if we *are* the coping mechanism?
crawl across bodies, through the hour—collect
the chaos of memory and the chatter of senses.

TAW & JSC
JULY 14, 2020

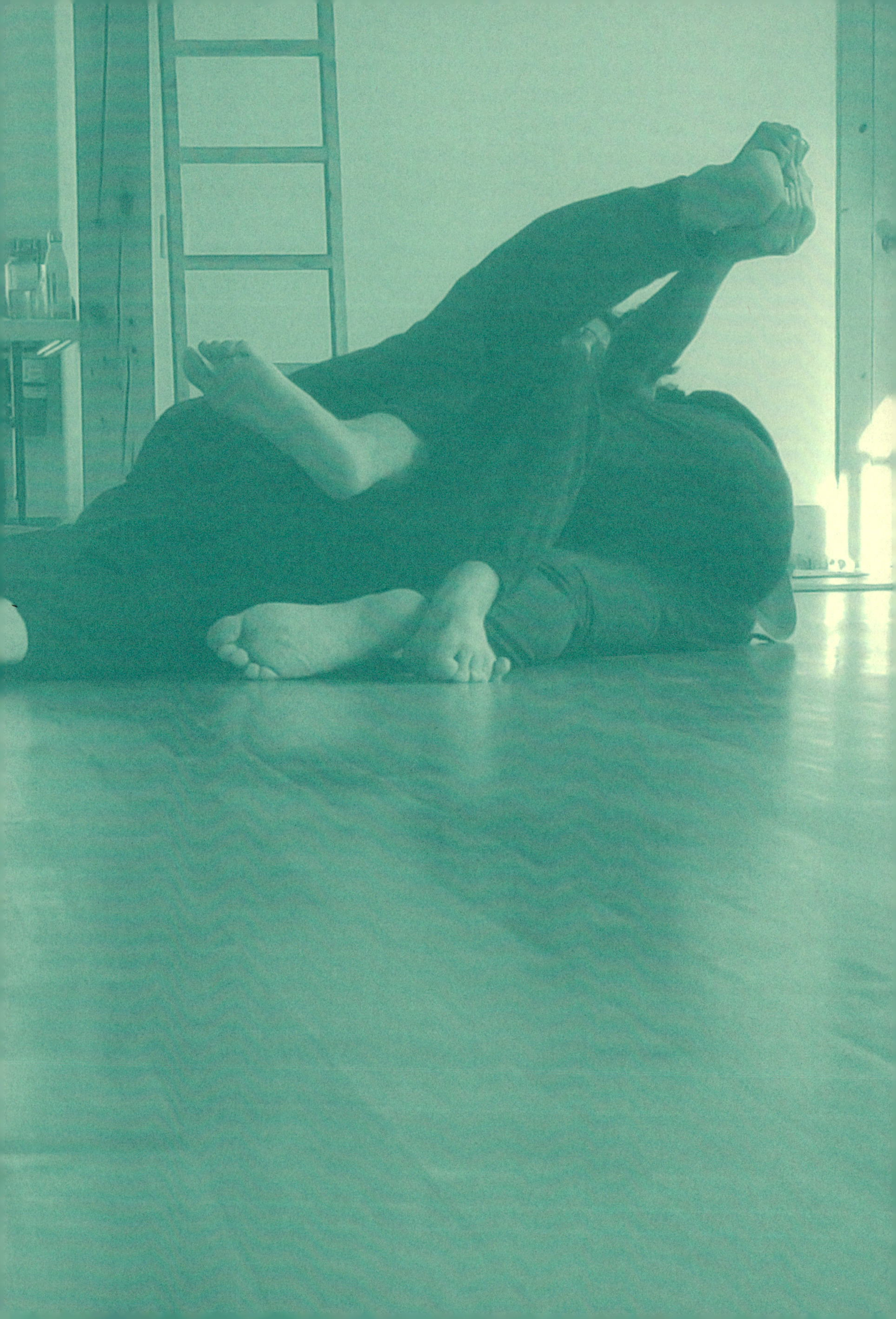

MARKING THE OCCASION

MARKING THE OCCASION

Edited by
Jaime Shearn Coan and
Tara Aisha Willis
in collaboration with
Dorothy Lin

Published by
Wendy's Subway

CONTENTS

CONTENTS

A Map, a Frame, a Moving Archive

Jaime Shearn Coan and
Tara Aisha Willis

Tara and I met in a graduate seminar, but we could have met just as easily at a performance. Tara is a dancer and writer; I have performed a bit but have also been involved in dramaturgy and, when I was writing reviews regularly, I was usually in a collaborative relationship with the dance artists I wrote about. In 2015, we were asked to serve as writers-in-residence for the Movement Research Festival held at Mount Tremper Arts in Upstate New York. A couple months later, we started collaborating in earnest at a residency at Mount Tremper, curated by AUNTS. We weren't assigned to work together, we just did. We gathered stacks of books (mostly related to performance theory, poetics, and Black studies), placed two pieces of butcher paper on tables, and moved back and forth between them, writing in response to each other's words, as well as to quotations we'd selected. We read the text together for an audience at the end of the week. This was the first time that writing as an action—and performing that writing for an audience—entered our conversation. The question of how to write together keeps coming up in Jaime and my collaborations, cross-hatched with questions about writing as action and meaning-making in movement that can only be answered by *doing* both (and everything in between).

I remember a hurried meeting with Tara in the cafeteria of the Museum of Modern Art (museums! remember museums?). We were writing in a shared Google doc, as usual, trying to articulate our vision for the Watershed Residency at Mount Tremper Arts. It was at this meeting that we stumbled into the title *Marking the Occasion*. It was slow going. The concept came out of our long-standing desire to experience more intersections of writing and performance—beyond the review, the scholarly article, the score, the artist statement, and the grant proposal. We wanted time to experiment with other performance-based artists grappling with these questions. We started thinking of the residency, with its duration and requisite performance, as a place to stage our questions. We wondered, "Can a performance be a rough draft of a written work?" Thinking of a publication as the "goal" or "final movement" of the residency, we hoped to offset the traditional arc of developing a performance and to instigate different trajectories for live work and text. In forming a group, we wanted to move beyond our own subjectivities in favor of a multiplication of lived, embodied experiences, with artists from across the country who occupy multiple roles within performance economies, who make performance work in which language and writing are prevalent. We wanted individuated practices to be brought into our shared studio and exchanged, and we hoped that collaborative practices would emerge out of the group through spending time together.

Once we arrived back at Mount Tremper in July 2019, the largest portion of our week was spent on "practice-shares": each of us led the group for an hour, inviting text and movement into interaction. As we went, we took photos of each other in the studio, audio-recorded our speech, and shared pens, butcher paper, books, markers, sticky notes. The latter ended up covering the wall: a way of pulling ideas from all of our practices and placing them into a shared toolkit, into visual configurations. We attempted to spin our gathered practices and processes into new ones, combining versions of the shared "scores" into hybrid new ones, or doing them in tandem or sequentially. Aside from the amazing dinners provided by the chef, the other key structuring element of our week was the three set times each day at which a bell rang; everyone would go to a notebook and write for ten minutes. The notebooks were set up in six locations: Firepit, Garden, Living Room (two notebooks), Studio, Studio Loft, and Porch. Everyone dropped into writing at the same time, from different positions within the enclosed world of the residency, responding to their immediate environment as well as to the contents of the notebook, and creating a collaborative writing practice, across space and bounded in time.

Having initiated and dreamed up this situation, Jaime and I knew our roles would be first curatorial, then editorial; we were also participants/performers during the residency. How to balance the holding/hosting work of curator and editor with the creative and generative work of being within the thing itself? Or were those false dichotomies? I remember the questions that came up when we explained the shared notebook practice to the group. We were all beholden to this rigid writing rhythm, an order within changeable, drawn-out days, but we each adapted it to ourselves and the moment. Jaime and I tried to be timekeepers, schedule-shapers, process-nudgers, direction-providers. At the same time, we were (sometimes overly) careful to avoid the feeling of aiming "towards" something. It's challenging to move things along, while attempting to be fully enmeshed within what's happening—and prepared to let it fall into a new shape. We were inside of and guiding what felt a lot like a dance-making process, while trying to not actually make a dance.

Near the end of the residency, Jaime and I revisited our original description of the project to adapt it for the performance's program notes. Without changing the language much, we switched it from future tense to present tense: from "we will" to "we are." No longer hypothesizing the experience, we were now trying to frame the ongoingness of the residency alongside the presentness of the "final" event. Our prediction that *new practices will emerge out of the group through spending structured and unstructured time together* had simply become an ongoing fact. The trick was to keep the final event, the occasion of the performance, feeling like a continuation of that experiment rather than the culmination. Against all our attempts to diffuse its centrality, it was an ever-present pressure.

The loose structure that we decided on for the showing was to activate the shared practices in an improvisational score, hoping to reveal an embodied archive of our time together while adding to that archive. But what happens when you include a softly structured lighting design and an audience? The feeling of needing to determine our technical needs, to figure out the configuration of the audience, to delineate a way of beginning and ending, of transitioning between elements: these expectations set up by the event-ness of it all shaped our process during the last couple of days. The texts we wrote to propose the project and then to explain it to our audience indicated a lot about what the performance event *wasn't*, but not much about what it *was*. Which is, perhaps, the only way to fully escape the primacy of *the occasion.*

A year later, Tara and I began the process of making the proposed publication with Wendy's Subway, working closely with their staff and our designer, Dorothy Lin. We wanted the book to serve as an extension of the residency as well as an archive of it. We hoped the archive, including the notebook, photos, and ephemera, could be put to use for new readers and new contexts. We issued fairly open-ended calls to the residency participants, inviting them to respond from where they each were at within the life-altering reign of the pandemic and the uprisings in response to the systemic subjugation of Black people in this country. That is to say, we wanted to archive *this* time as well. Tara and I are wary of reinforcing the supremacy of the written archive, as both of us have prioritized performance as archive, the body as archive, in our work. This stance is shared by the contributors as well. We hope that a sense of the body—surviving, struggling, joyful, ambivalent, solitary and in relation—is sustained throughout these pages.

The yellow pages of this book hold the contributions by each of the artists, with interstitial (or adjoining) text from Jaime and I—residues of our residency, our co-writing practice, and our holding/hosting role in the group, all filtered through the present moment. The white pages hold an incomplete archive of the notebooks we shared over the course of the week. While the entries were written at designated times of day, they were inconsistently initialed and dated. The archive is divided by the location of each notebook, and entries are provided in the order in which they appeared in the notebooks. That order is not precisely chronological, as some writers skipped ahead or chose to annotate other entries. Many of the pages included are referred to or repurposed in the contributions, and where possible they have been cited by location/notebook name, writer's initials, and page number.

Just as we wanted the performance to be a continuation of that week of shared practice, this book is as well. But it is also a finale. The process and performance in 2019, and the time in between then and now, in 2020, are all enfolded in this book, which is an archive, which is a publication, which is a performance. There was an occasion, and now there is a collection and reworking of those moments and durations, on paper. The book could be read as an event: with its own arc, a relationship with time and action and bodies. But there are other occasions being marked here, too: the ripple effects of a pandemic in a country whose seams are full to bursting with structural violences that long precede—and will continue long after—the moment our performance ended last summer and the moment you are reading this book.

JSC & TAW
AUGUST 2020

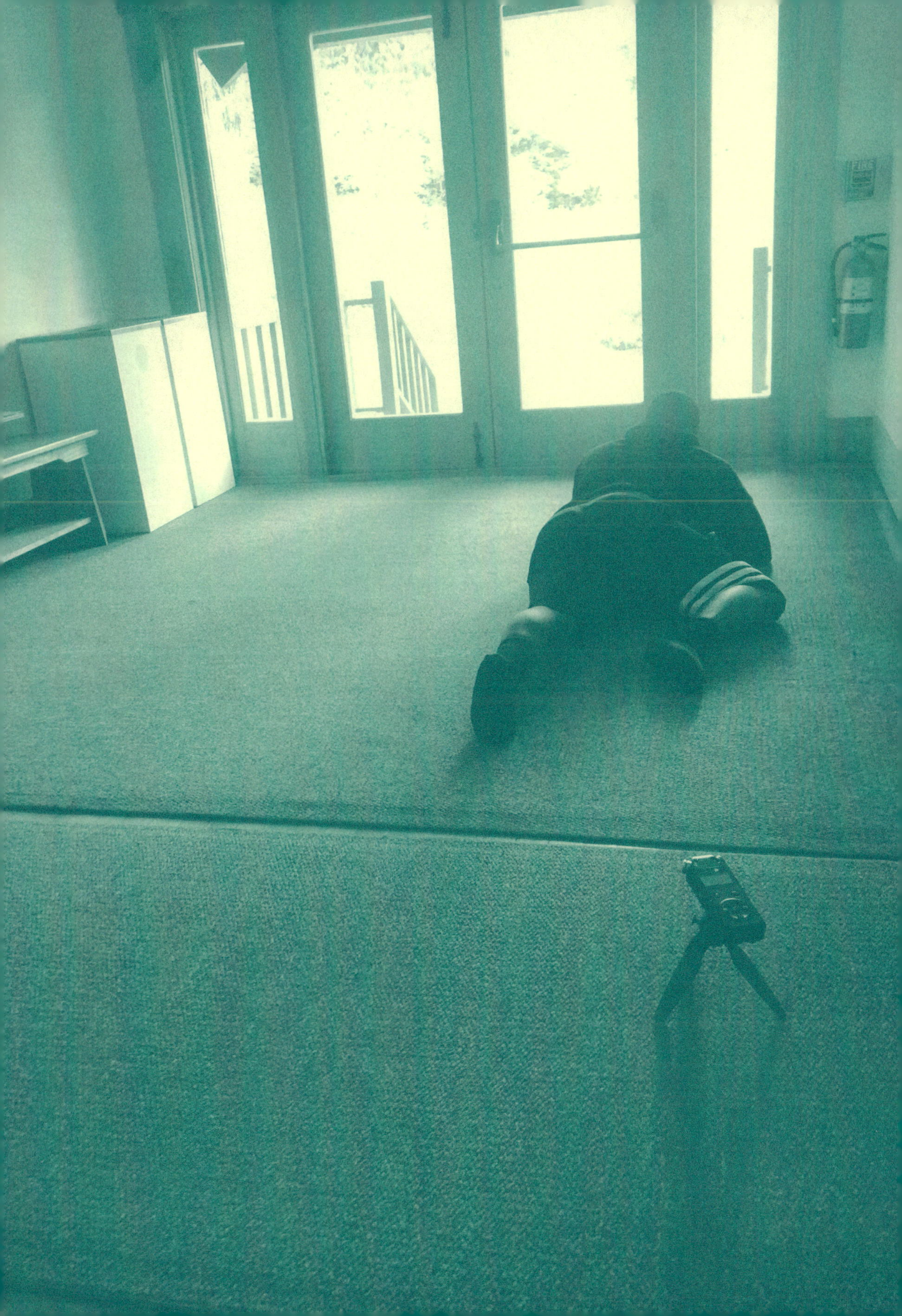

listening

(to eachother
to sound
to space
to self
to absence|silence|gaps)

People have been painting murals on boarded up windows in SoHo. They read: BLACK IS BEAUTIFUL. MY EXECUTION MIGHT BE TELEVISED. GOD IS A BLACK WOMAN. BIG BUSINESS IS KILLING US! FREEDOM ISN'T FREE. Layers upon layers, growing more meaning every day. The movement from protecting property to protecting bodies. Keeping connections intact. The plywood is claimed as a field for communication. It keeps speaking when the protestors go home to rest. Listening happens virtually so much these days. It gets flattened, reconstituted, disembodied. In the crowd, we remember vibrations—the relationships between sound and space. We feel the resonance in our chests and the prickle on the tiny hairs of our arms. Names are expelled from the inside of our soft bodies and they collect in air, multiple, floating above us. Repetition is a felt unforgetting.

JSC
JUNE 23, 2020

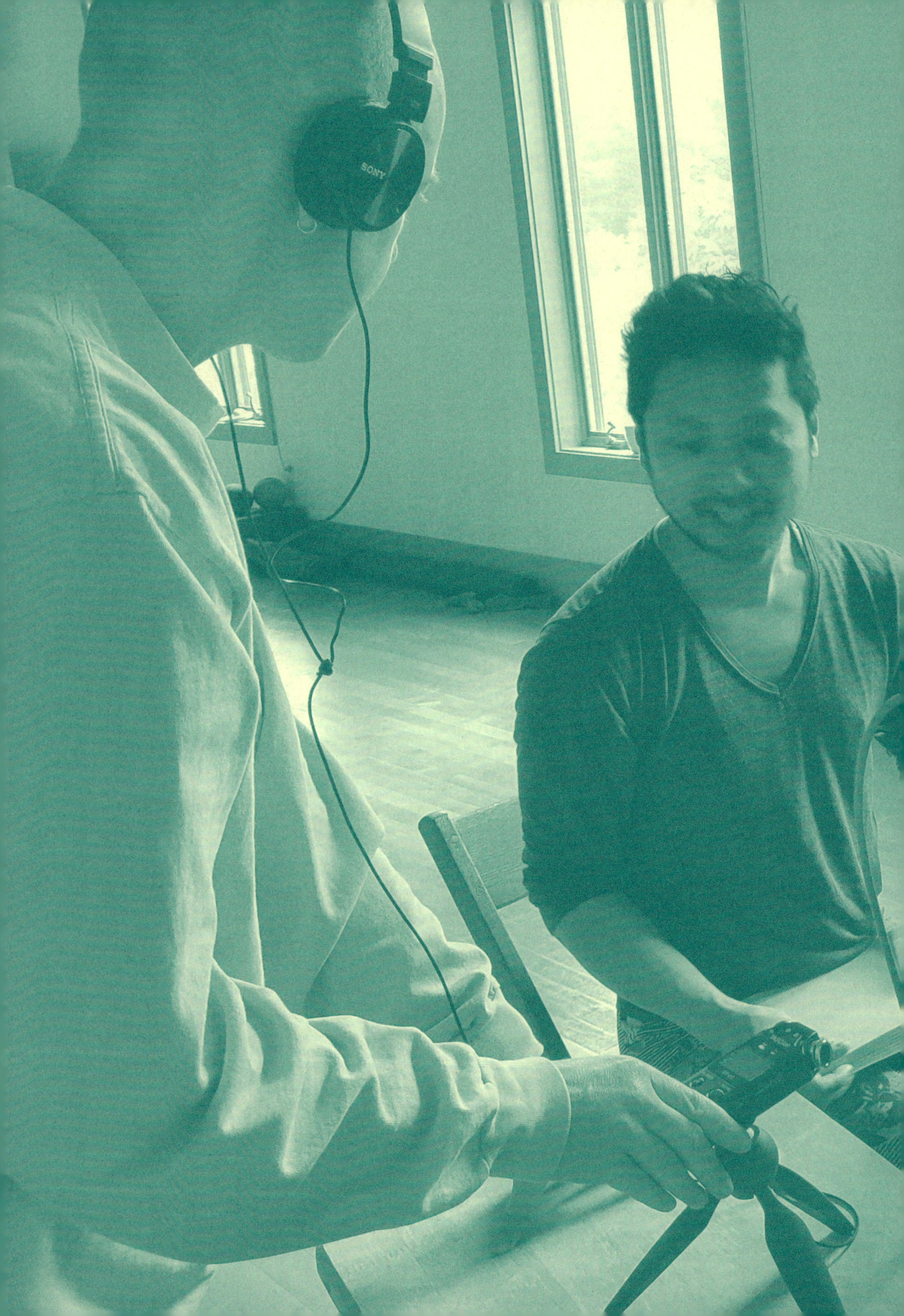
SONY

Arrival

Mariana Valencia

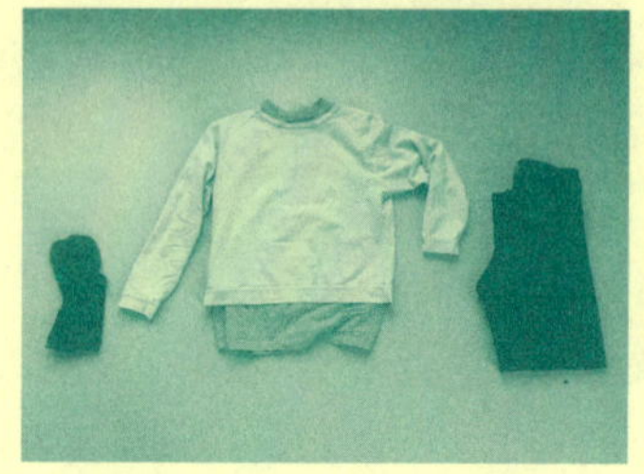

FEBRUARY 6, 2020

Dark gray socks, pink mauve sweatshirt layered over an ochre t-shirt. Black canvas high-waisted pants.

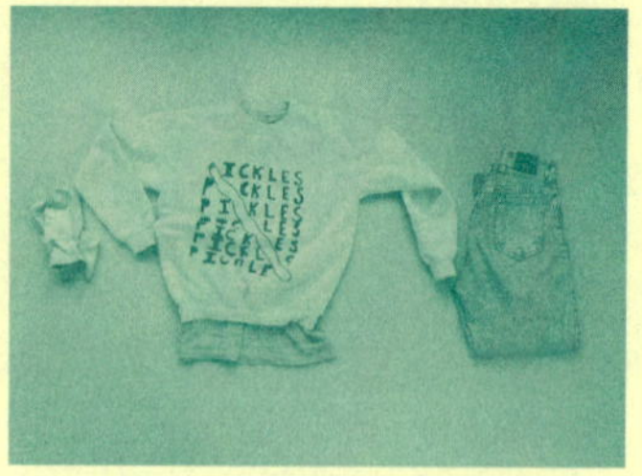

FEBRUARY 7, 2020

Light gray and white striped socks, neon pink sweatshirt with “Pickles” screenprinted in black seven times. The repeated word makes a block of text and across the text in a bold diagonal is a screenprint of a long pickle. Ochre t-shirt layered under. Vintage acid-washed jeans folded twice over at the hem.

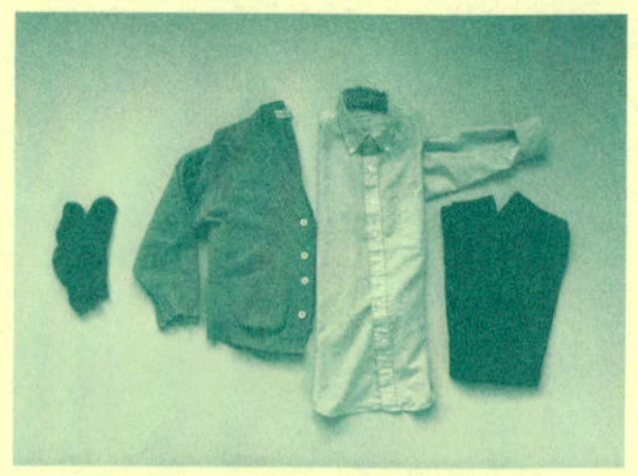

FEBRUARY 11, 2020

Dark gray socks, brown wool cardigan with ivory white buttons layered over a light blue oversized men's dress shirt with white buttons. Black leggings.

I make dances that I choreograph in dance studios. Dance studios are typically rented by the hour and I bring everything I need for those hours into the studio and take it all away when my time is up. The unofficial mindset is: leave every dance studio better than I've found it, like a campground. It's beyond good manners; it's about respecting the community of artists who bring life into the space.

When entering a dance studio, I take off my clothes of the day, lay them on the floor to air out, and change into rehearsal clothes. On the floor, my clothes of the day can breathe, and freshen up because my commute marks them with sweat—I tend to run hot. The clothes I choose to wear in the morning are composed for the activities of my day. My clothes of the day mark the occasion of my arrival to rehearsal and later a meeting, an appointment, a dinner, or an art opening. My clothes of the day are colors, materials, and textures for any eye to capture and gaze upon for even just a moment—in New York City, this can mean many gazes in a day. My clothes of the day let gazes rest when gazes need to be held; a visual code, the armor that I carry through each hour.

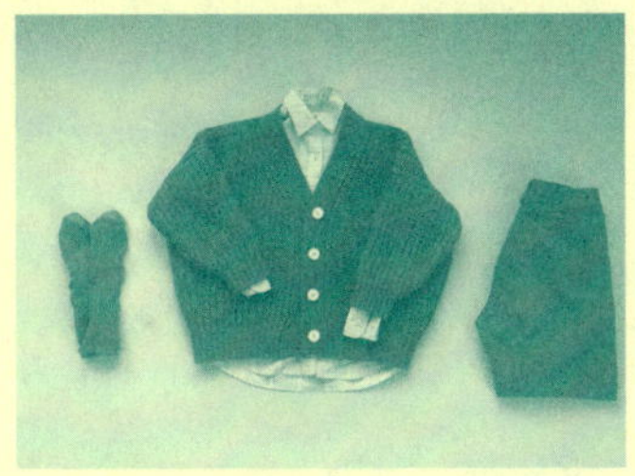

FEBRUARY 12, 2020

Ocean blue socks with yellow detail at the toe. Lapis blue wool cardigan with white buttons layered over a women's dress shirt in mint green, pink, and gray plaid. Army green canvas high-waisted pants.

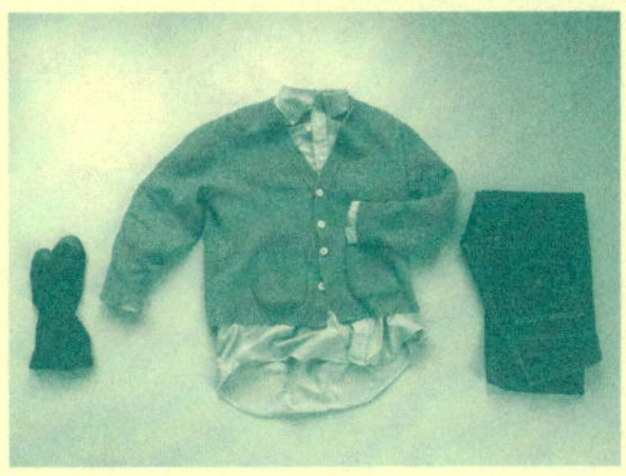

FEBRUARY 13, 2020

Navy peony blue socks with yellow detail at the toe. Brown wool cardigan with ivory buttons layered over a light blue oversized men's dress shirt with white buttons. Black denim jeans with gold stitching.

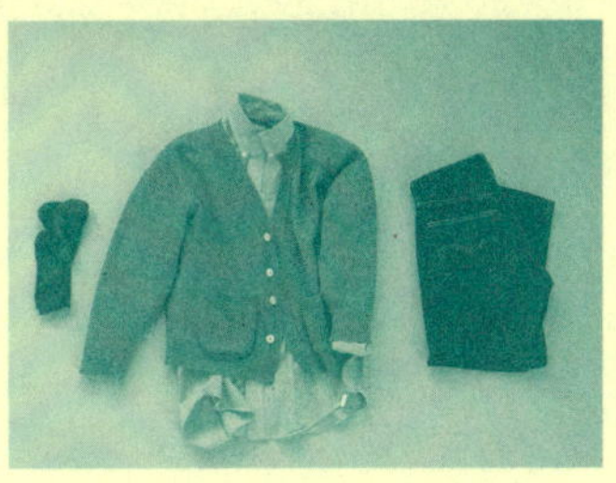

FEBRUARY 14, 2020

Navy blue socks, brown wool cardigan with ivory buttons layered over a light blue over-sized men's dress shirt with white buttons. Black denim jeans with gold stitching.

The garments I wear to rehearse in are imprinted by my body because I've spent active sweaty hours in them. A raggedy set: a saggy legging, perfectly worn sweatpants, an old t-shirt, a soft sweatshirt, and various sock options. Rehearsal clothes are better than clean clothes because of the markings that my body makes onto them; their fibers are ready to receive me time and again. My studio practice always begins with this transition and in this threshold. My body shifts from the outer world into an inner world.

I make dances in dance studios alone. I've been a solo artist for some years now but I enjoy collaboration, too. During the week in the studio at Mount Tremper, I work with Taka, Julie, Mlondi, David, Jaime, and Tara and my transition into that studio is the same: I change into sweatpants, an old t-shirt, sometimes socks. We share our practices with each other, each donning soft imprinted clothes through which we activate space in unison.

When Julie leads us in her practice called "The Pressure," I find myself bearing people's weight and lifting them upward whenever I receive

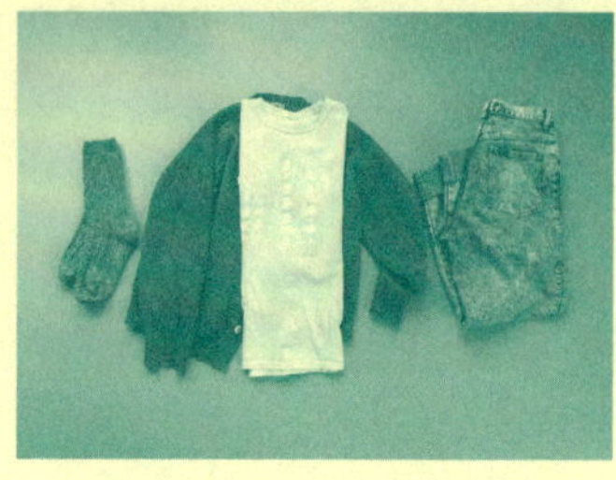

FEBRUARY 25, 2020

Amber yellow and black heathered socks. Brown wool cardigan with ivory buttons worn open over a white t-shirt with the word "GAY" silk-screened in white. Vintage acid-washed jeans folded over twice at the hem.

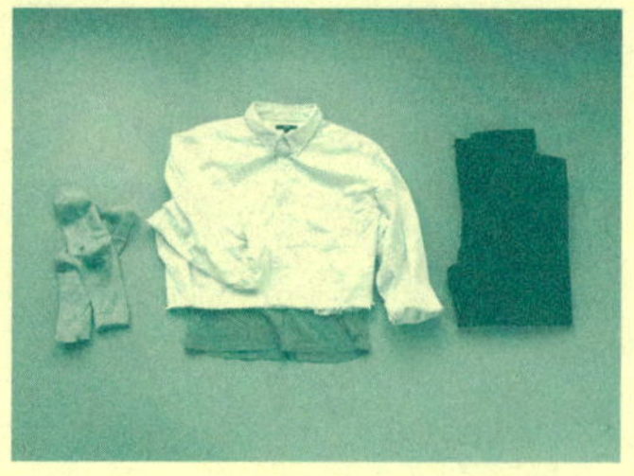

FEBRUARY 26, 2020

Salmon socks, brilliant white denim button down shirt rolled at the sleeve, cropped and slightly frayed at waist. Raspberry red t-shirt worn under. Dark blue denim high-waisted pants with yellow stitching.

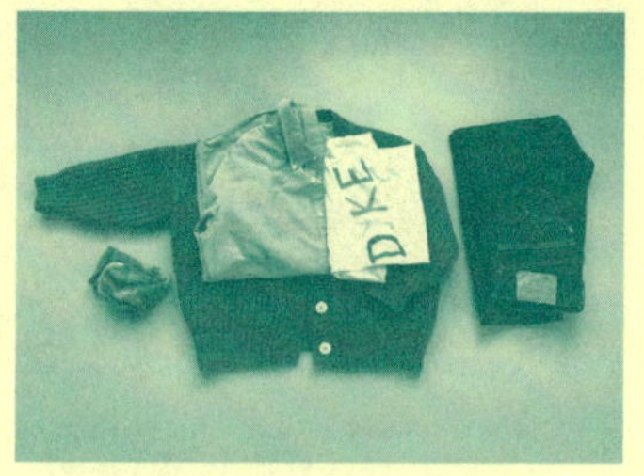

FEBRUARY 27, 2020

Garden green socks with white enforcements at the toe, heel, and arch. Lapis blue cardigan with white buttons layered over a light blue oversized men's dress shirt with white buttons. White t-shirt with the word "DYKE" silkscreened in blue, yellow, red, and green worn under. Black denim jeans with gold stitching.

the weight they give. "The Pressure" is a practice where two or more people press into each other, at times partially, at times through a wrapping of bodies. It is a practice of intention and physical impression. "Lift up the ones who need lifting. Lift up through gravity. The gravity is in each of us. DO YOUR PART." (PORCH, MV, p. 164)

A year has passed since the week at Mount Tremper, and within that year, our lives are changed, having experienced so much loss in all directions; each person on the earth feels a shift. The pandemic shows us that societal structures are built to oppress us; the vulnerable are more vulnerable and the privileged question why they suddenly feel jeopardized, too. Like "The Pressure," it is time for our collective friction to make us feel each other with intention.

At Mount Tremper, I hear the gunshots of hunters in the countryside: "It's interesting to hear gunshots in this countryside. My sister hears them all the time in Chicago. She says that each week, there is a tally of all the people who have gotten shot that week or weekend, I cannot remember which. In any case, last week or weekend, 28 people were

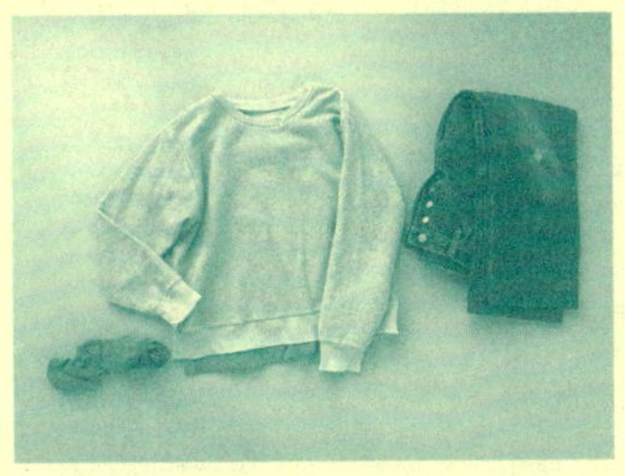

MARCH 2, 2020

Niagara blue socks. Moonlight jade sweatshirt layered over an olive green t-shirt. Classic denim blue jeans, threadbare at the knee.

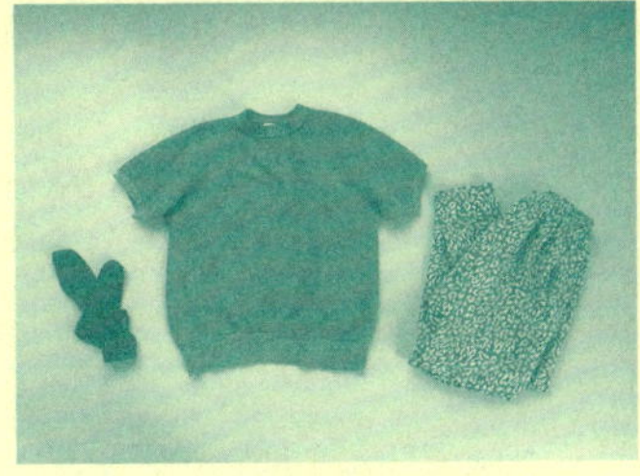

MARCH 3, 2020

Dark gray socks, cool gray heathered short sleeve sweatshirt, cool gray leggings with rosewater pink leopard print and emerald green pocket detail.

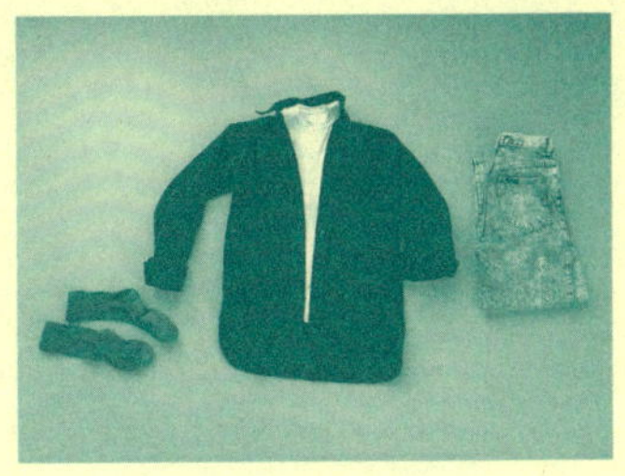

MARCH 4, 2020

Ocean blue socks with yellow detail at the toe. Cobalt blue flannel button down shirt with pockets and buttons sleeves rolled up and worn open over a white t-shirt with the word "GAY" silkscreened in white. Vintage high-waisted acid-washed jeans.

shot in Chicago." (PORCH, MV, p. 163–164) I wonder if in the countryside, there is ever a tally of gunshots, too; in either case, the gunshots toward the hunted haven't stopped.

It's 2020: We shout against systemic violence and the centuries of injustices that the pandemic has woken us to. The system has stopped and a new energy is moving; the underbelly shouts.

It's 2020: I have a studio residency on Governors Island in New York City from February through June. As soon as the residency begins, I rehearse as often as I can; the room is all mine to make dances, write, and read in. The studio looks out onto the Hudson and East Rivers, Manhattan, and the Statue of Liberty. I have access to the studio up until the pandemic shuts us down in March, and though the pandemic interrupts the completion of my residency, I'm able to look back at a tiny side project, a photographic journal that documents my clothes of the day on the floor of my studio. What you see here are the photographs translated into words describing my clothes of the day at my studio on Governors Island almost a year after my

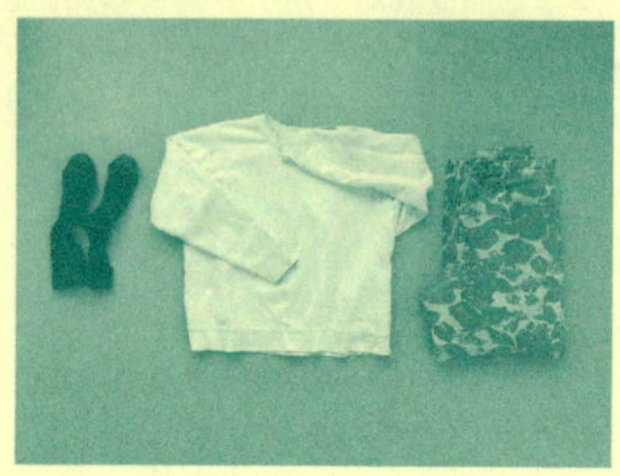

MARCH 5, 2020

Navy peony blue socks with yellow detail at the toe and bright white sweatshirt. Baby blue vintage jeans printed with ultra violet purple roses and teal green leaves.

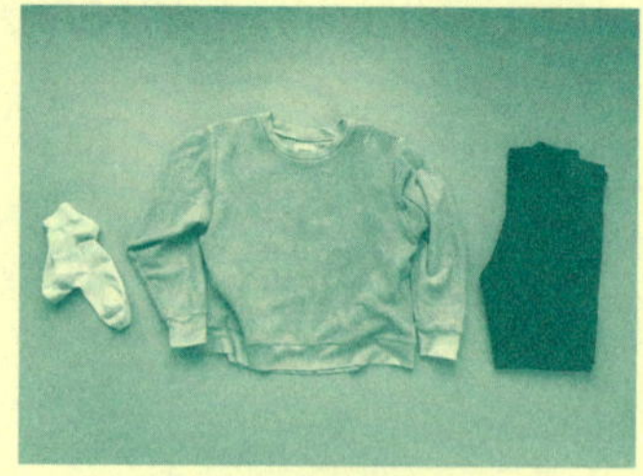

MARCH 10. 2020

Vintage white ankle socks. Moonlight jade sweatshirt. Black high-waisted jeans.

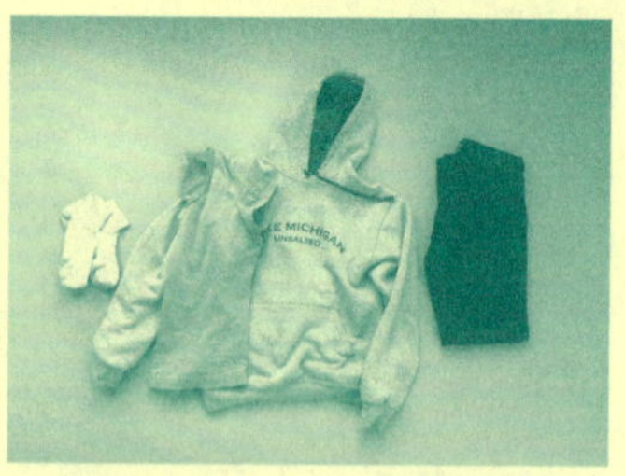

MARCH 11, 2020

Brilliant white ankle socks. Heathered glacier gray hoodie with cool gray tie and hood lining, the words "LAKE MICHIGAN UNSALTED" screenprinted across the chest. Abbey stone t-shirt, black highwaisted jeans.

time at Mount Tremper. The descriptions are the transition threshold, retelling the marks of my arrival to the studio. There is some sense of embodied loss in the descriptions.

It's 2020: Loss is immeasurable, and suffering degrees of loss in unison creates a spectrum of immeasurability that is hard to grasp; people have died. On a personal level, I can't go to the studio anymore, I can't convene with friends in the studio either, but I'm still alive so I can still put on clothes, and maybe even go outside to pick up groceries, to catch a breath, and today, to attend a protest. When I enter my home now, I take off my outside clothes carefully (there might be contagions on them) and I change into my inside clothes; my transition ritual from rehearsal has shifted to this new version of the threshold. The reason for changing my clothes is different, but the action is the same. A simple act that marks the occasion of my arrival, a daily ritual, alone yet still together.

MARCH 13, 2020

The pandemic brings rehearsal to a sudden stop on March 13, 2020; I'm unsure about how to adapt my studio practice, but I answer the call just as well. My daily embodiment echoes my writing at Mount Tremper: "When someone says *you are finished* it's different from feeling *done*." (FIREPIT, MV, p. 114)

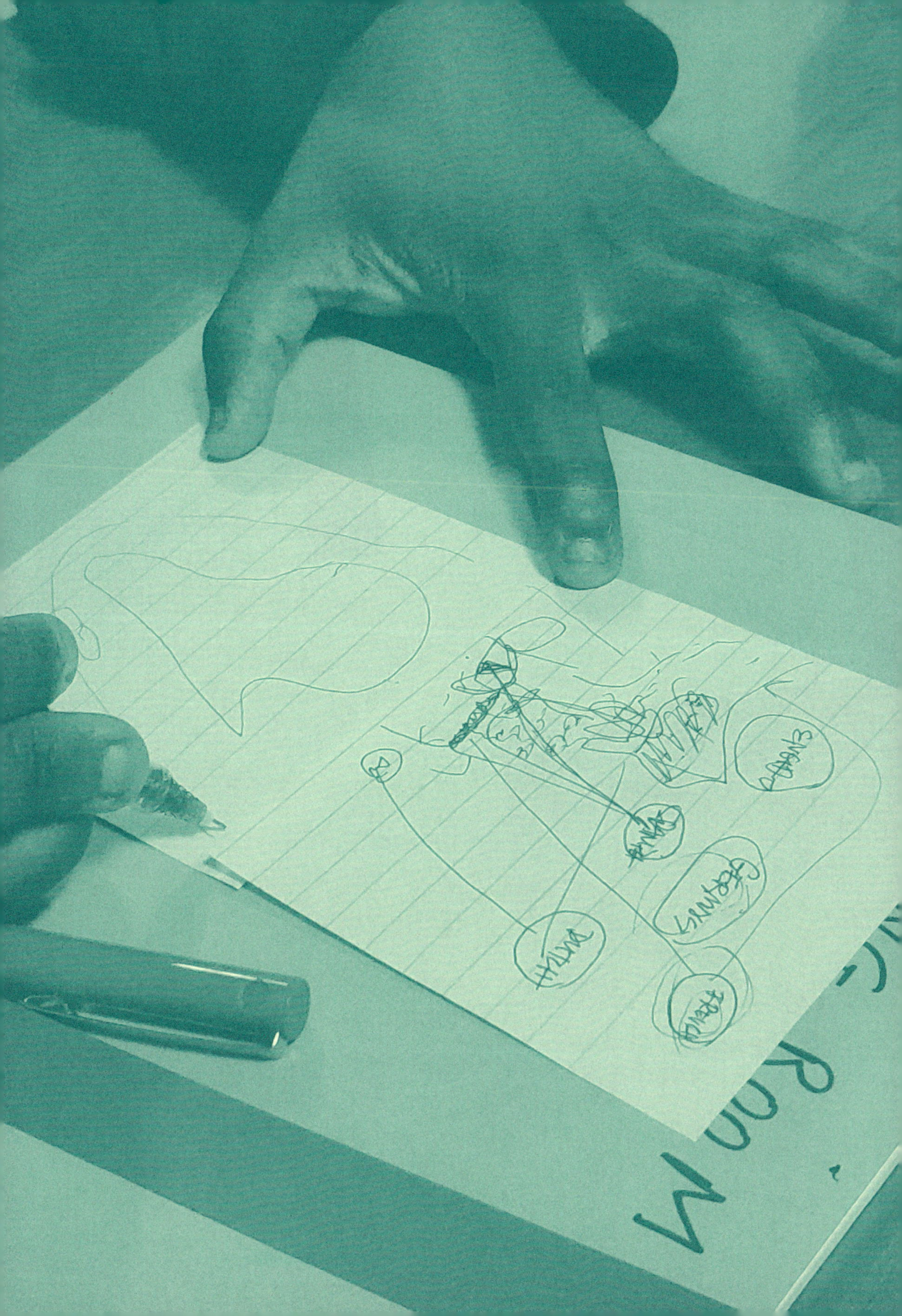
ROOM

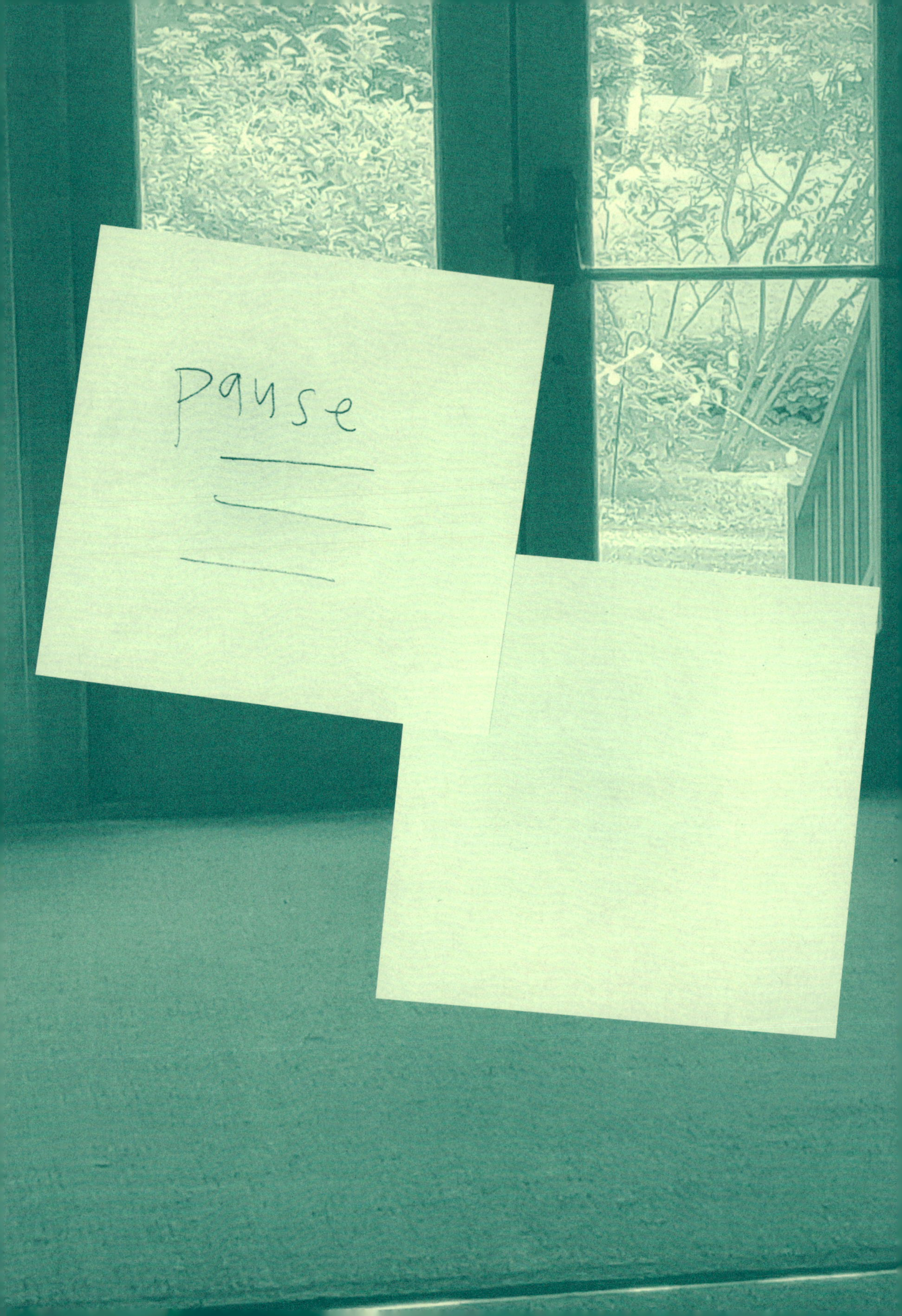
pause

Being in the same room for days, weeks, months on end attunes us anew to the changing light and cycles of weather—how the rain feels differently on a cold sharp day or a heated summer evening; how the sun goes down against the tree outside in March versus June. The duration of a day has gone strange. Still familiar, speckled with tasks and meals and scheduled meetings, but now the time it takes to cross the city each day is replaced with or augmented by the time it takes to get out the door with hands washed, mask on, sanitizer in pocket, route mapped to avoid crowds, waiting in line to enter, and time set aside on the return trip for cleaning off your groceries and undoing all you've done. Except there's no undoing this mess. No unraveling this intricate weather map of violent systems touching and tracing each other across our history to get us here. There is only the living—living it hard and lovingly into a new shape and hoping others will do the same with you, or perhaps even more so. All this, because the days are really centuries, generations, and sitting here along the timeline at its end (for now), you are tired.

TAW
JUNE 24–25, 2020

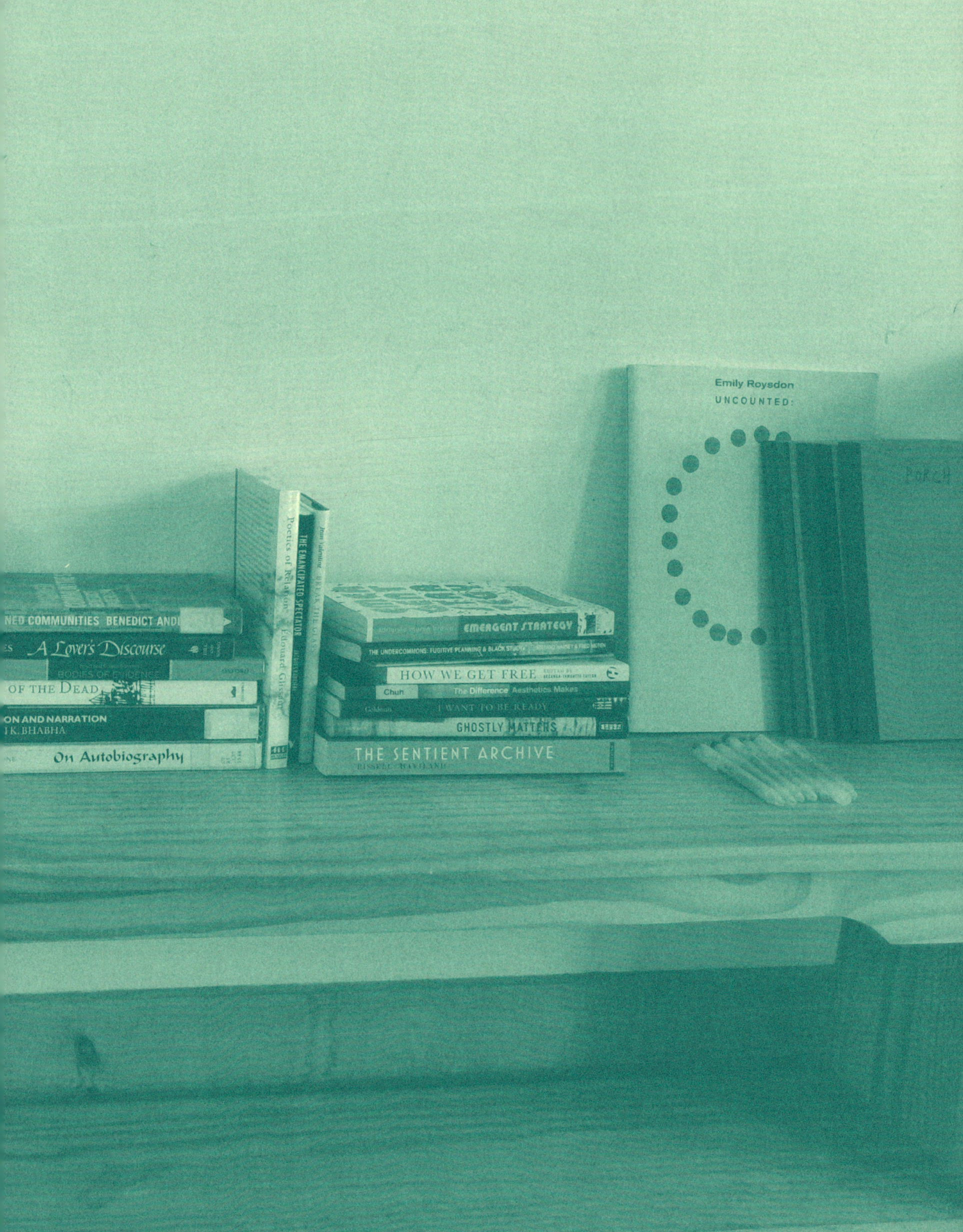

Emily Roysdon
UNCOUNTED:
NED COMMUNITIES BENEDICT AND
A Lover's Discourse
OF THE DEAD
ON AND NARRATION
K. BHABHA
On Autobiography
Poetics of Relation
THE EMANCIPATED SPECTATOR
EMERGENT STRATEGY
THE UNDERCOMMONS: FUGITIVE PLANNING & BLACK STUDY
HOW WE GET FREE
Chun
The Difference Aesthetics Makes
I WANT TO BE READY
GHOSTLY MATTERS
THE SENTIENT ARCHIVE

The How of Memory

Takahiro Yamamoto

In the past year or two, the ungraspable yet extremely palpable concept of "time" has been on my mind. In addition to physiological and ontological inquiry and the historical association of the sun/moon cycle to chronological measurement, I have been mainly contemplating the subjective and emotional effect of time. How does time influence the way I see the world, or the way I acknowledge who I think I am? Shuffling through writings about time by multiple thinkers, it seems that our capacity to *remember* things is at the core of our perception of time. Although each of their approaches differ in various ways, they all somehow always come back to memory.

I feel complicated about memory. I always have. It is because I am often caught between my desire to cling to past feelings and my distrust for the accuracy of my own memory. Why do I remember only certain things and not others? Is my past experience less valuable if I don't remember it?

In the summer of 2019, we all were gathered at the beautiful Mount Tremper Arts. At the tail end of our time together, I posed this question to David Thomson: “Could ‘relations’ or ‘relationships’ be a form of time?” As I sat down on the dance floor in the mid-afternoon under a cloudy sky, I quickly jotted down several thoughts that came out of his mouth in response.

I reviewed my notebook on the bus ride back to New York City to note, in red pen, what I could add to what I wrote at the moment of that conversation. As I look at this page now after a year has passed, I have only a vague recollection of most of the ideas and information I had written. Somehow, the original question doesn’t hold much interest for me anymore. But one line caught my attention, a question which David raised as he looked directly at me after taking a slight pause: “How do we remember things?”

We did a lot of writing and moving at Mount Tremper. I believe there was an underlying interest in the potential yet unlikely alchemy between dancing and writing. Both mediums are time-based, relying heavily on memory to experience them. However, the difference between them lies in the ability to mark their trace. Writing *is* the markings left behind. Dance's markings disappear immediately. I truly cherish the different natures of both mediums. I keep coming back to them in tandem to explore the same thematic concern in my projects; however, I deliberately do not vocally narrate or digitally project my writings in my performances. I find that using them as separate routes of investigation works better for me. I want some ideas and experiences to have an ephemeral life and others to have longer traces, allowing me and the public to come back to them again and again for further contemplation.

Writing provides a sense of permanence and proof just like photography. But even if things are written down, they are not always relevant or important. I don't even believe in what I write sometimes. As I jot quickly in my notebook, it is inevitable that some things are left out. In an essay, my original thoughts and feelings, through multiple rounds of rewrites and editing, start to fade out and eventually become something more polished and shaped.

06/18/19 Working with DHT TIME

Q5 · Relations / relationship as a form of time

· visibility

· "Quietly political"

· Ambiguity abstraction : power of dance. power of body
complication

· time is a marker of relationship

We put value on it.

Seeing "relationship" through marker of value in time
quality of time.

Sense of time — what you do with the time

density

duration

Takahiro Yamamoto

6/18/19 Working with DHT T/ME

Qs · Relations / relationship as a form of time
· visibility.
· "Quietly political"
· Ambiguity ~~and~~ abstraction : power of dance. power of body
complication
·

time is a marker of relationship

we put value on it.

Seeing "relationship" through marker of value in time.
quality of time.

Sense of time — what you do with the time
Density
[reverse].

then mess them all up.

Arc of ~~being~~ beginning and ending.

Buddhism exercise on fertility. Beans separately.

How do we remember things

Circadian time.

Light... ← changing the rhythm of life. ← candle

Cycle of the moon - gravity. women's cycle?

low & high tides

Einstein's relativity. ← speed. time.

Mortality. FGT.

Circadian rhythm: 24-hour internal clock. sleep/wake cycle

Go to 77

As I reflect on my experience at Mount Tremper, I want to bring back David's question: *"How do we remember things?"* Particularly on this beautiful occasion we had together last summer, thinking about the "how" of remembrance brings up the connection between that specific point in time together and my subsequent interactions with everyone. After we parted, I got to see Tara, Jaime, Mlondi, Mariana, Julie, and David in various modes of engagement in different locations, such as witnessing live or video performances, texting, dancing at a party, rehearsing for my project, or just hanging out. Every time I get to interact with each of them, some memory is conjured: a random image, a smell or sound from the time at Mount Tremper, an utterance of thoughts, or the way that person hugged me—but in a different shade, through a slightly noisy or translucent filter, or in the way that you focus the camera in and out. Here I am, typing these words on my computer and thinking about each of them right at this very moment. And, yes, I am experiencing this phenomenon: not being able to confirm which memory was true, which feeling was projected, or what imagery was skewed.

I forget and leave things out to remember certain other things, and vice versa. My forgotten things might show up later unexpectedly or create space for something else to be conjured up *in a different shade, through a slightly noisy or translucent filter, or in the way that you focus the camera in and out.* Maybe this analogy applies to the process of writing as well. It can consist of what was written, what did not get written, and the potential that lies in between the written words. My past thoughts, which are left as conscious or unconscious traces, provoke emotions and meanings according to where I am mentally and emotionally at the time of rereading. And, I'm finding value in the spark of provocation that emerges out of what I thought I remembered. As I sit with this impermanence of memory, I am beginning to think about memory as a combination of what I remember and what I forget.

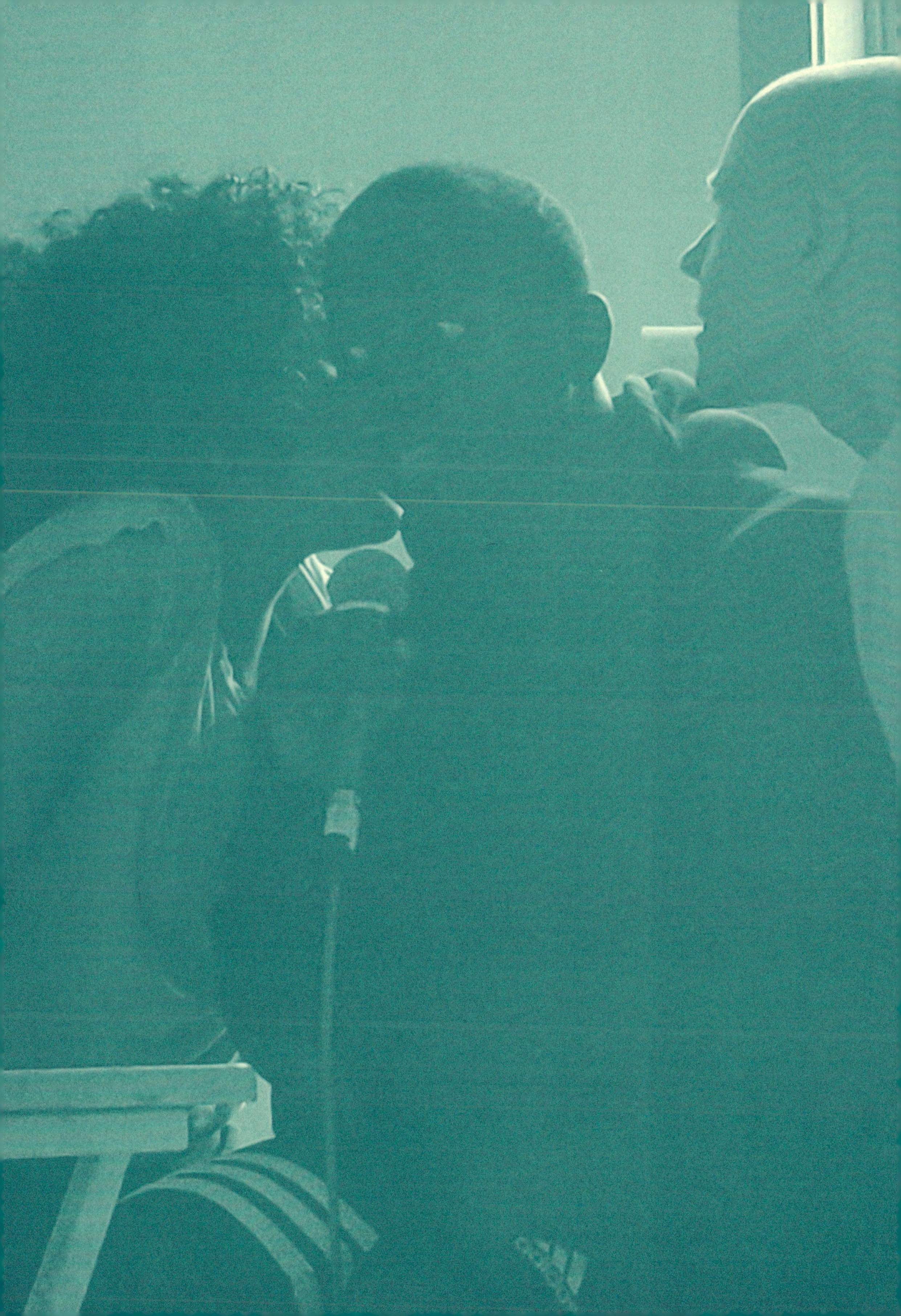

whispering

(as intimacy
as mode of communication
as conspiracy
as privacy
as quietude
as gossip
as sound)

Early in the morning, everything at whisper pitch. With the whisper, you take it for granted that you can't capture it all, that you receive only fragments, bits of dreams and overheard conversation. A whisper might soothe, it might incite. It is what we're doing here, speaking to each other in soft tones, from far away, and waiting for the other to catch on to a word or sound that sparks. In the practice, two people whispered into one body at once. The one body tried to make sense. As we always do. In what direction do your words tend? Towards interiors or wide-open spaces? Years ago, I made a book called *dear someone* where I asked people to write anonymous letters, whispers. Something about distance and intimacy. As I write now, I hover above a timeline that will shortly send me 3,000 miles away. Intimacy threatens to crack. I am told to put a hand on my heart and whisper to myself what I need to hear, in the midst of the whirling. Small children love to cup their hands and whisper into the ear of an adult. The most mundane observation becomes a revelation. Or perhaps it remains and has always been a nonsensical sound. In the cover of night, I can whisper my fears, let them get lost in a field of warmth, which is a way of saying, the beloved.

JSC
JUNE 26, 2020

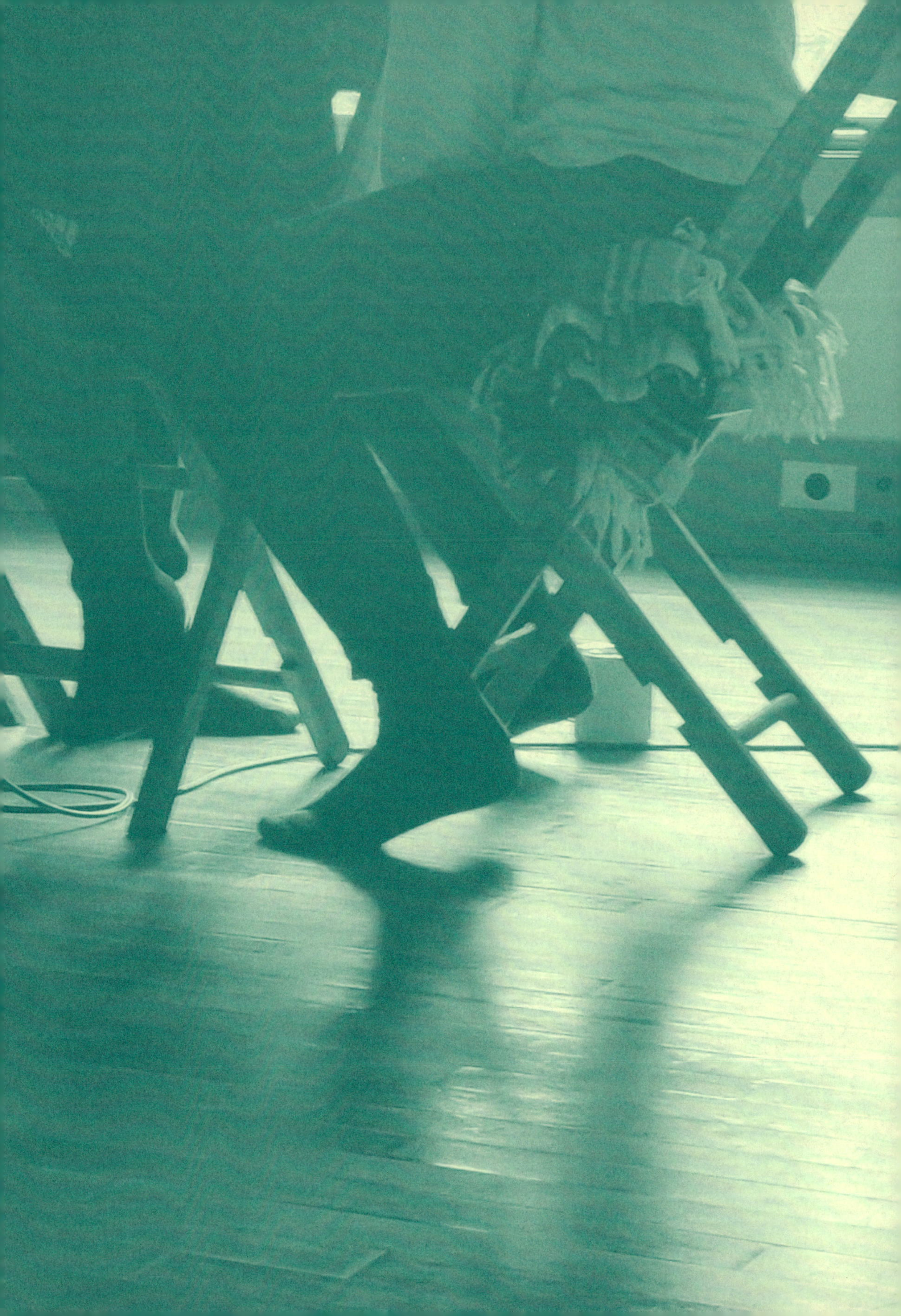

a negative operation
(on "nature" and capture)

Mlondi Zondi

participants in my practice share were invited to go out (or in), to lean into what they consider to be "nature" and think creatively about how they were going to "capture" that, or narrate it to everyone. i was intrigued by definitions of "nature" that are reducible to organic matter only. for example, i chose to photograph a lot of black rubber and black plastic (shaped in the circular form). rubber and plastic are not usually considered "natural," or at least those are not the first things people gravitate towards when they think about nature. rubber and plastic are processed, but why do we exclude what is processed from our idea of "nature"?

this question is very related to artistic practice, especially in the context of artist residencies that are situated in secluded areas "close to nature." oftentimes you hear people saying that natural landscapes unlock their creativity. what is the relationship between "nature" and creative stimulation? why are artists so interested in "nature" as muse? the skyscrapers in Manhattan are not not nature (they are made with materials that come from the earth, some of which are processed). the hope was that these provocations would help us all think critically about (and perhaps let go of) the expectation that "nature" be our creative muse (this is an old, partly anthropocentric problem. think European Romantic paintings that tried to "capture" landscape, and certain aspects of land art). the goal was to let go of assumptions about what constitutes nature. the Land ("nature") in the Americas is not "unprocessed." the ground we stood on and danced on, the ground that fed us, has a history of colonial plunder, Indigenous genocide, slavery, etc. how do you participate in a residency in a landscape such as Mount Tremper and not romanticize "nature," since that romanticization is an active forgetting of "nature" as also carrying centuries of bloody memories? i planned this practice because my biggest source of anxiety prior to coming upstate was comfortably reverting to the tenets of art historical eighteenth- and nineteenth-century Romanticism.

ultimately (and this correlates with my journal posts), i was extending my general practice, which is all about foregrounding a negative operation. this entails an insistence on negative thought and affect/emotion as opening up certain kinds of possibilities in terms of making/moving/thinking/sensing. I was trying to open up a space where we could work from negative/killjoy questions, and really think about what has been negated (historically) for our practice to take place. a negative operation fetishizes neither process nor product. i realized that a workshop such as this one requires more time.

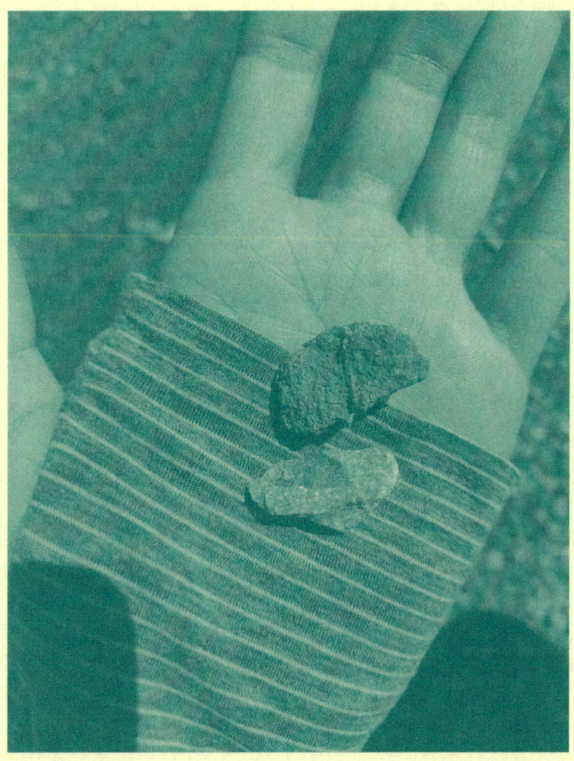

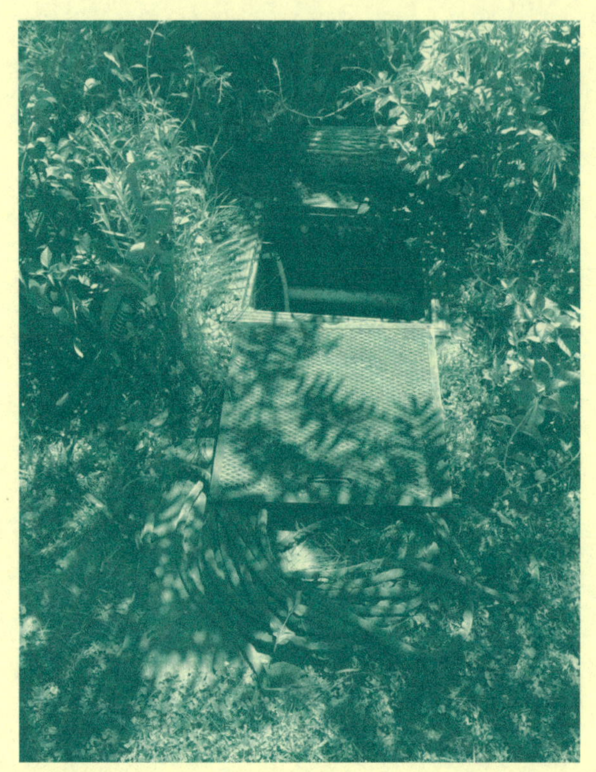

not there.
This morning is that repression.
This morning is that consensus
This morning is that hegemonic common sense.
This morning is that ~~collecting~~ collective and wilful forgetting.
This morning is facing the monster dead in the eyes
This morning is cowardice
This morning is obfuscation through art.
This morning is not mourning
This mourning is the refusal of mourning.
This mourning is false identification
This morning is precious bruised feelings.
This morning is that violence of sentimentality.
This morning is the cooptation of blood work
This morning is I embarrass you
This morning is capitalist feeling
This morning is healthy paranoia
This morning is did I do something wrong
This morning is am I too excessive
This morning is how much abrasiveness is allowed.
This morning is the erotic
This morning is anti-capitalist tenderness
This morning is if I could love you
This morning is catachresis for what I can't call love
This morning is I see you
This morning is that feeling
This morning is we don't do it
This morning is we're doing it
This morning is fail
This morning is failure is good is the reason why
This morning I am engulfed and engulfing
This morning is oh my god I did this thing this would be me would be doing this again would be transformed by this would be thinking this is right would be uncertain would be just right would be muscle memory would be what we would look like if we were free. — mlondi, 2pm, Wed, 12 June

A dance of listening. Listening, in and of itself as a dance

What does it mean to foreground a listening practice in dance process / composition / workshopping / making? I mean REALLY foreground a listening practice, rigorously, attentively?

Listening itself would be the dance occassion, about decibels vibrating from gut to gut. It probably would be frustrating, as on the surface it would seem like nothing is happening.

(John Cage approached this question in 4'42.)

If people came to see a dance and all that was, there was a listening dance, what would be the reaction?

The case we are making here is not about re-creating sound art (although there are clear parallels) More like LISTENING ART, ~~rather~~ rather than sound art.

(so what would shift perhaps is the perceived passiveness of listening.

(of course listening is always already active, even in our sleep.

Mlondi, 2pm
14 June

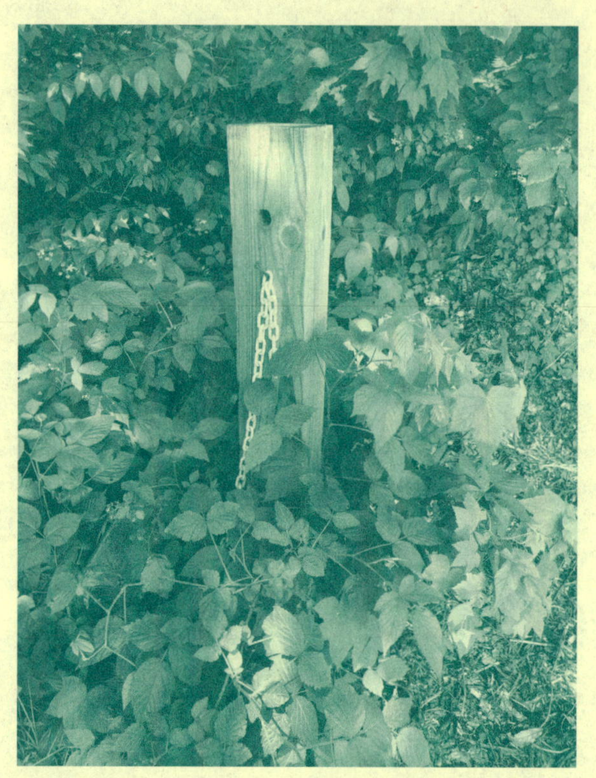

A Brief Letter to Queer Feminist Killjoys

The complaint is what we need. The complaint is the irritation we need. The complaint must be attended to without pathology or villification. The complaint must be listened to. The complaint sometimes cannot be heard, and in that situation, the complaint has to be addressed through the law. The complaint, in that case, is forced to valorize the law, the same law that kills the complainer. The complaint raises necessary sticky ugly feelings. The complaint wakes us up from the comma. Disneyland is not as shiny at the back. You don't see the sweat and the dust. Just the polish. Just the candy. The gingerbread pumpkin spice human-made snow. Romance. The complaint shows us the flaws of romance. The complaint teaches us about what we perceive excessive, too much, too extra, too wild, too emotional, a lot. The complaint is good (not in a moralistic sense) It generates alternative paths, encouraging us to slow down and re-assess. The complaint is creativity, is wanting more, is knowledge that more is deserved. The complaint bypassess cowardly, obliquity. It is the clarity we don't yet know we need.

*i am thankful to thinkers and makers/destroyers such as Ama Ata Aidoo, Sara Ahmed, FAKA, Lebo Mathosa, and Winnie Madikizela Mandela, for these thoughts.

Hell NO MANIFESTO

to doing
to candles
to just here
to the very least
to the managerial
to sentimentality
to showing
to thinking
to actually being . . .
to . . . . ing them
to attention
to the one who notices
to rot
to tumble
to reckoning
to guided by the stars
to the coming glory of the lord
to flinch
to writing
to not
to not
to not
to not
to never
to never ever
to the ~~moo~~ moon
to pressure
to the next item
to circumscribe
to knew this
to grinding
to ~~teeth~~
to other cavities
too precious
too productive
to generate
to withhold
to drift.

Mlondi Zondi 6pm

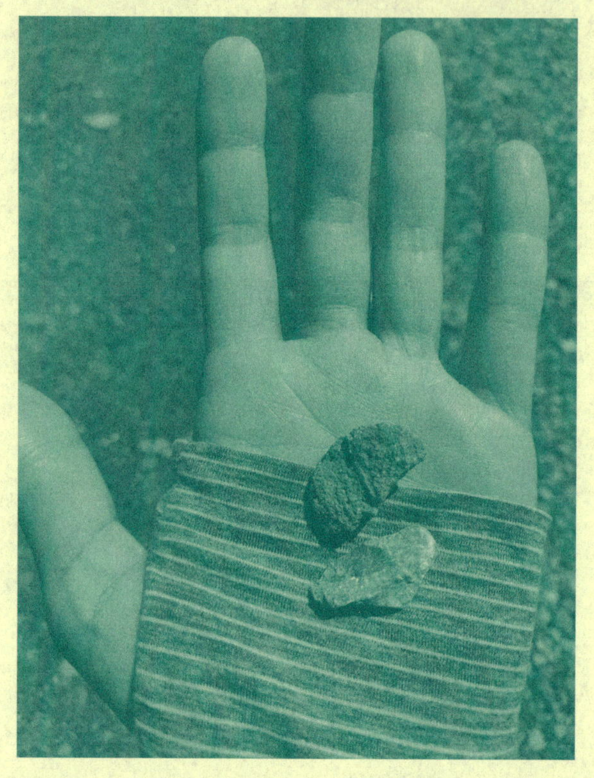

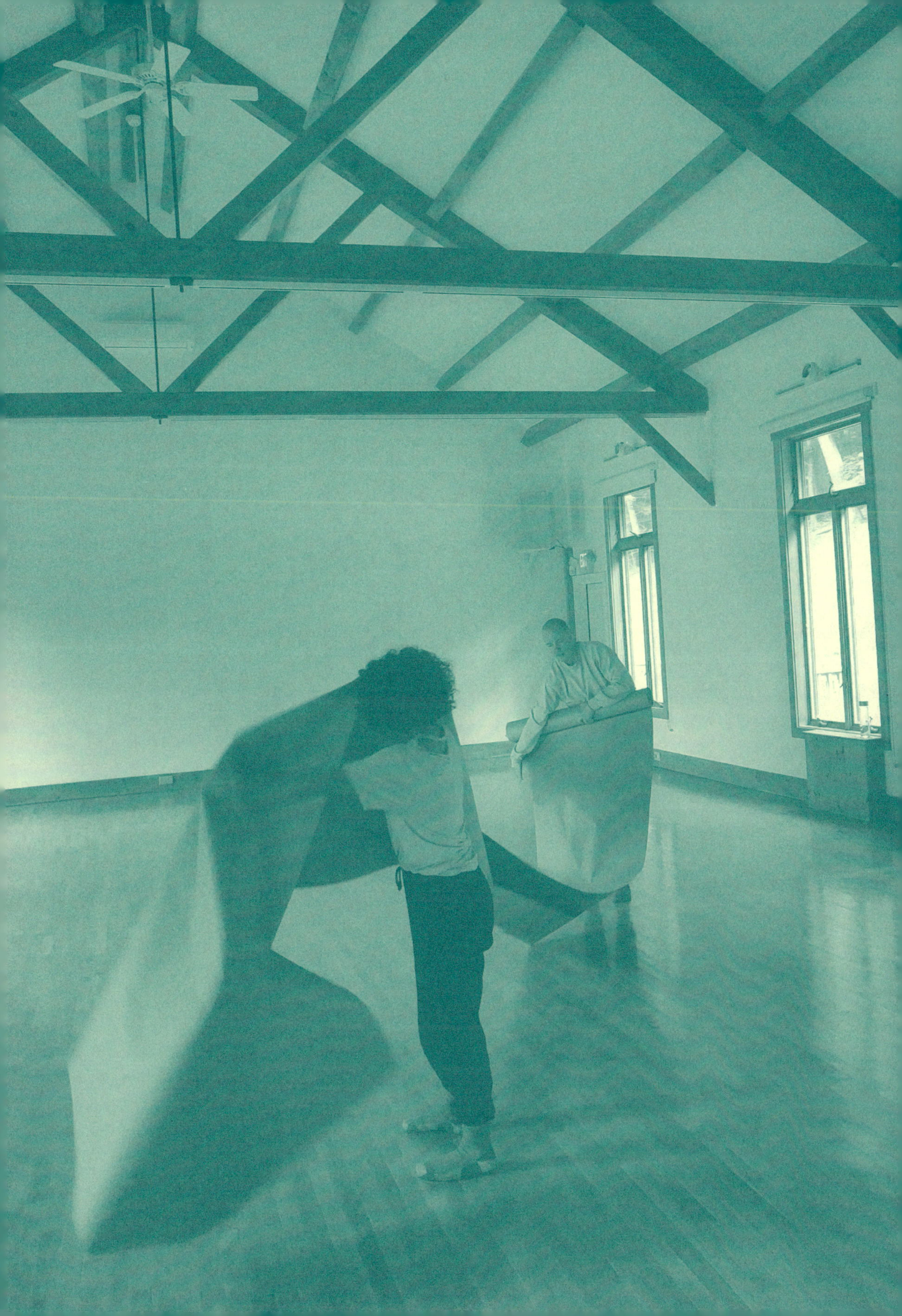

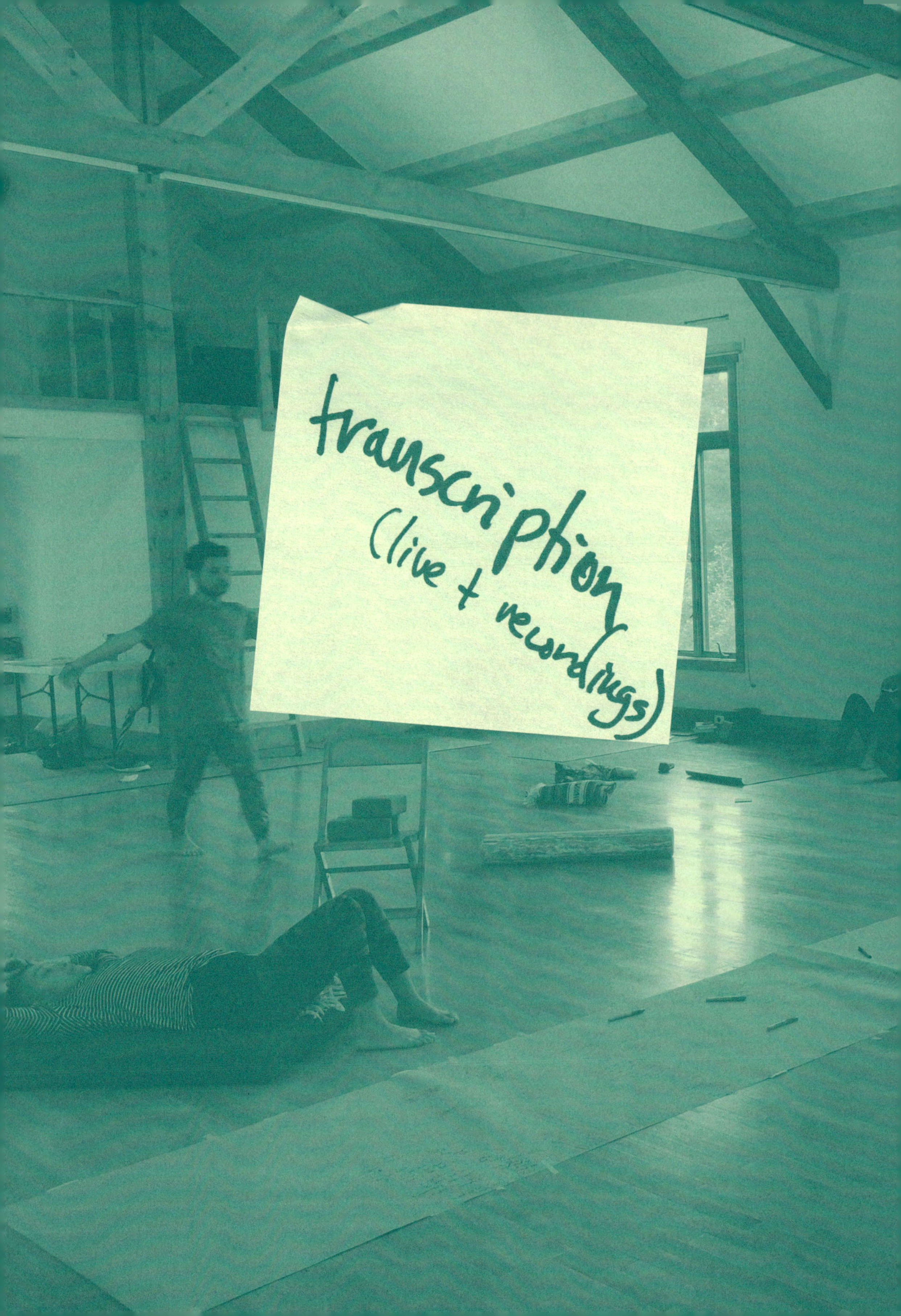
transcription
(live + recordings)

In the woods, on the side of a mountain, it's easy to feel a storm coming in. It rolls up the hill toward the tall studio windows, turning the sky from bright gold to silver-white and roiling to dark, with a purple or two tucked away in its curves. Across the wooden floor, probably, is a long sheet of butcher paper rolled out, cutting a shaft of even, dense brown through the center of the floor, that—probably—extends invisibly into the air like a curtain drawn across. An unspoken rule: the microphone (gripped tenderly by any one of us) and the hulking sound system hover stage right, while the rest of us hardly cross the divide cut by the roll of paper, even as we scramble along its chasm. We scatter language along it, probably, in serpentine or lumbering clusters. Any one of us alone with the microphone keeps pace with the racing clock, probably to fill the time sheepishly drawing out or to fit within it as it shrinks back from the details of the story we want to tell. The rest of us attempt to depict the hearing we're doing (and the seeing, feeling, empathizing, altering). It probably didn't storm that day, but the mountain rains, the writings, the microphones all congeal together between the repetition of those same four walls over days and the inconsistency of memory. Transcription as record? As description? As channeling? As impression? As incomplete and running out of hand-stamina or ink? As its own end, in itself, not a means for arriving at solid citation? As a surface to wonder across? As space (paper) and time (no repeats, no playback)? In workshops and rehearsals, I used to ask people to practice writing without looking at the page, while watching another person improvise. Palimpsests emerged, single words and phrases, layers and scribbles. How to transcribe a dance: not as a map for repetition or a record for legibility, but as a document of an experience—produced alongside the dance's doing.

TAW
JUNE 26, 2020

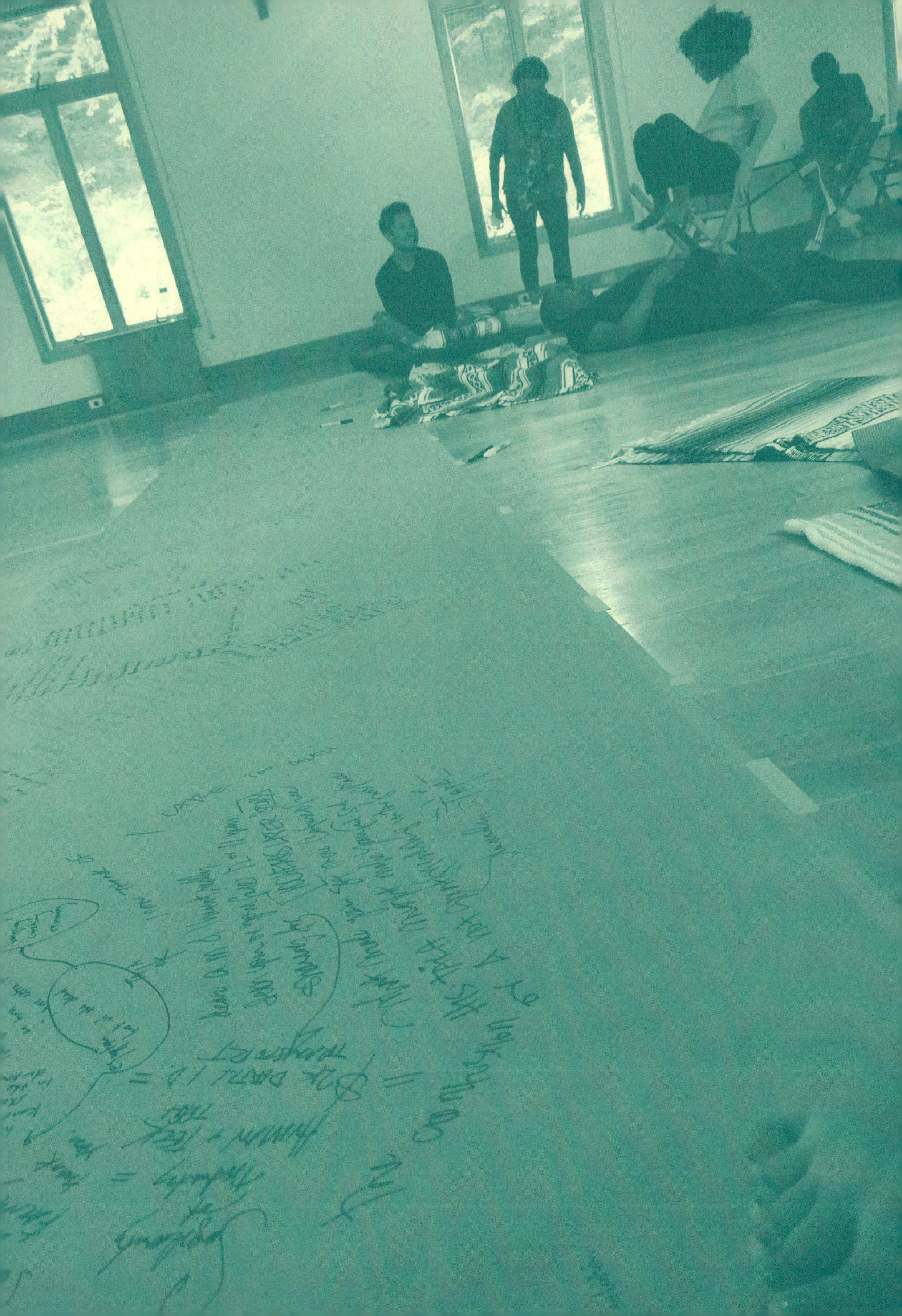

T–15
then
The Pressure
then
The Mic
then
Fern for the French Carribean
then
Dark Interior

Julie Tolentino

bear bear bear bear bear bear
generation choosing
rn nosty frosty frosty choosng time
cking clit clock watch watch ticking in no next

want to run.

Mostly away from this space, the foreign space differently in gesture.

It knows objects and surface friction. It knows interior and wear it like an old inside out

in space, and later,

to

The will to join in order to become the room. We may only iimagine with, or in the surrounding fluid.

(They have been teaching us this all along.

Does fluid hit with fluid or do the cells collide with each other at the pool's mouth?

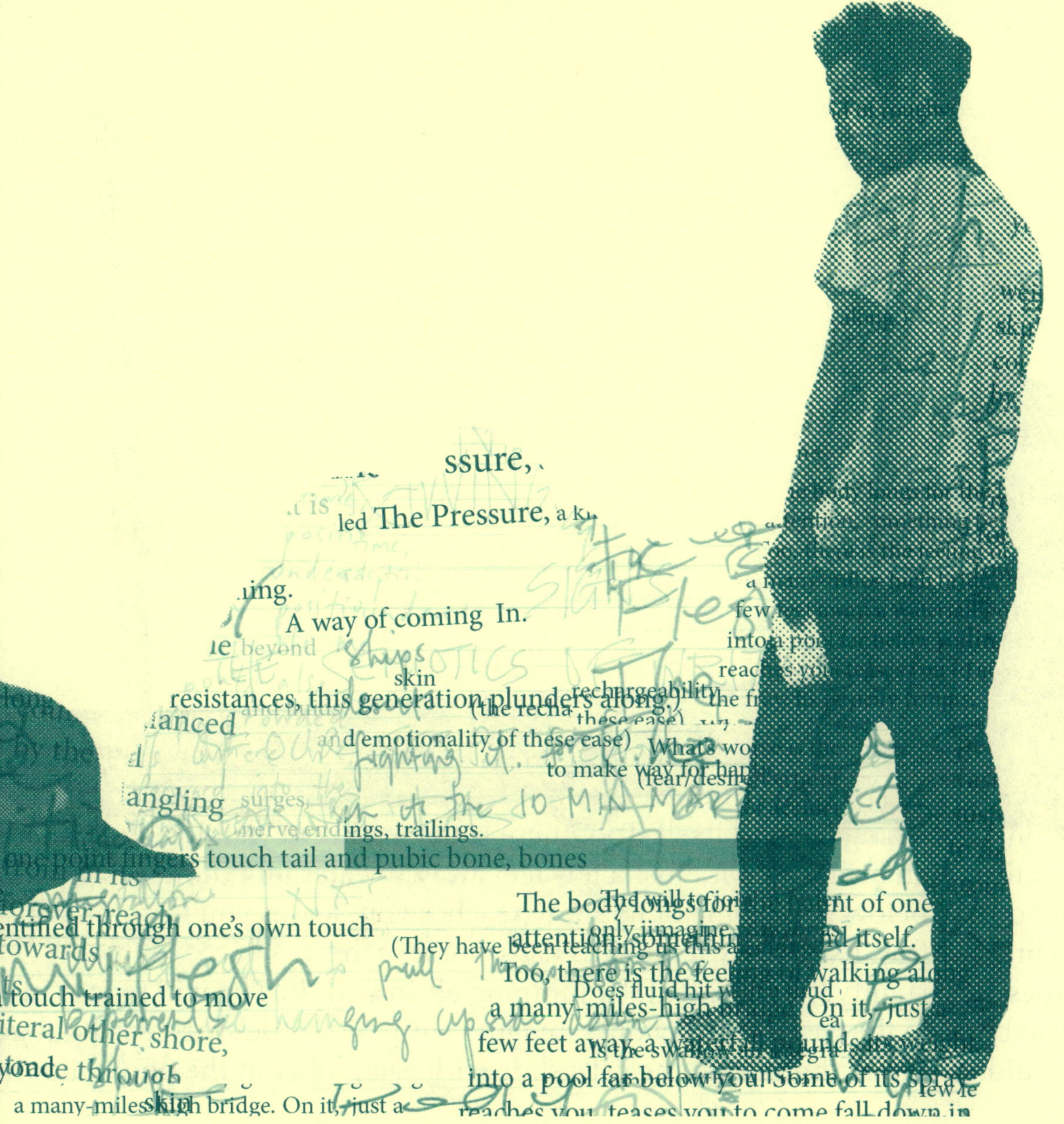

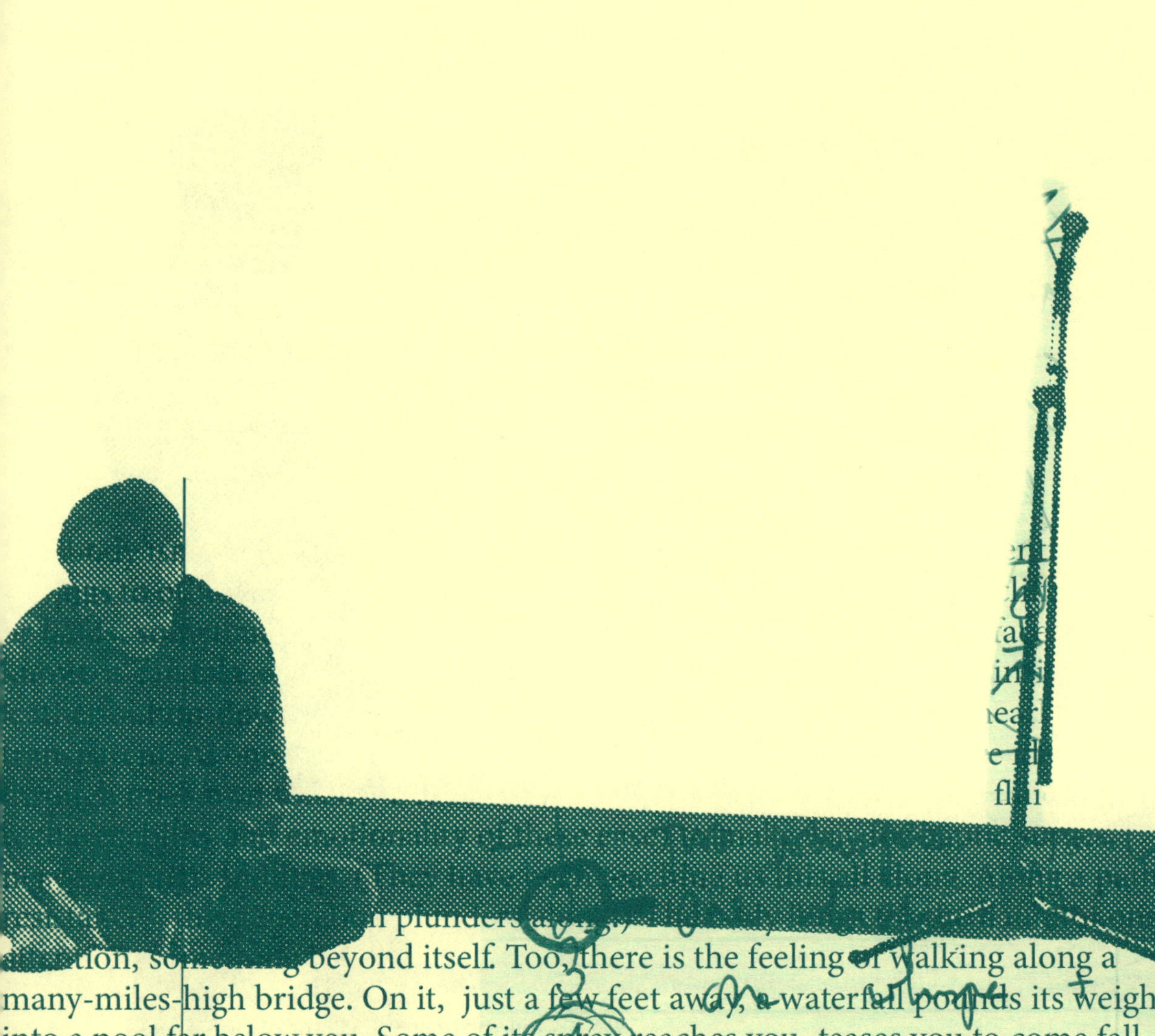

…tion, so… beyond itself. Too, there is the feeling of walking along a many-miles-high bridge. On it, just a few feet away, a waterfall pounds its weight into a pool far below you. Some of its spray reaches you, teases you to come fall down into the fray. Its ferocity tempts. What's worse is the ___ (fear/desire/certainty?) of accidentally jumping all-in with it. The will to join in order to become the rush. We may only imagine with, or as, the surrounding fluid Does fluid hit with a thud or do the cells slide with each other at the pool's mouth

mi... urns out, as it wants things and ... on. It
all the ... ularies that fall from some ot...
of lands, sometimes, in som... e's lap. It knows objects ... rface friction
knows it can take on its sli... terior and wear it li... old inside-out
leather button-down shirt ... n so... times that fi... nearly
transparent. At one poin... s touc... d pubic ... are identified
through one's own touc... ch... and fluids (the
rechargeability and ... s, ne
endings...
... haunt of one
... along a
... ts weigh
... me fall
...
(fear/desire/certainty?) ... oin in
order to become the rush. We may only imagine ... ounding flu
Does fluid hit with a thud or do the cells slide with each other at the pool's mout
Is the swallow an integration or a slap? Is that split a coming to or coming with?

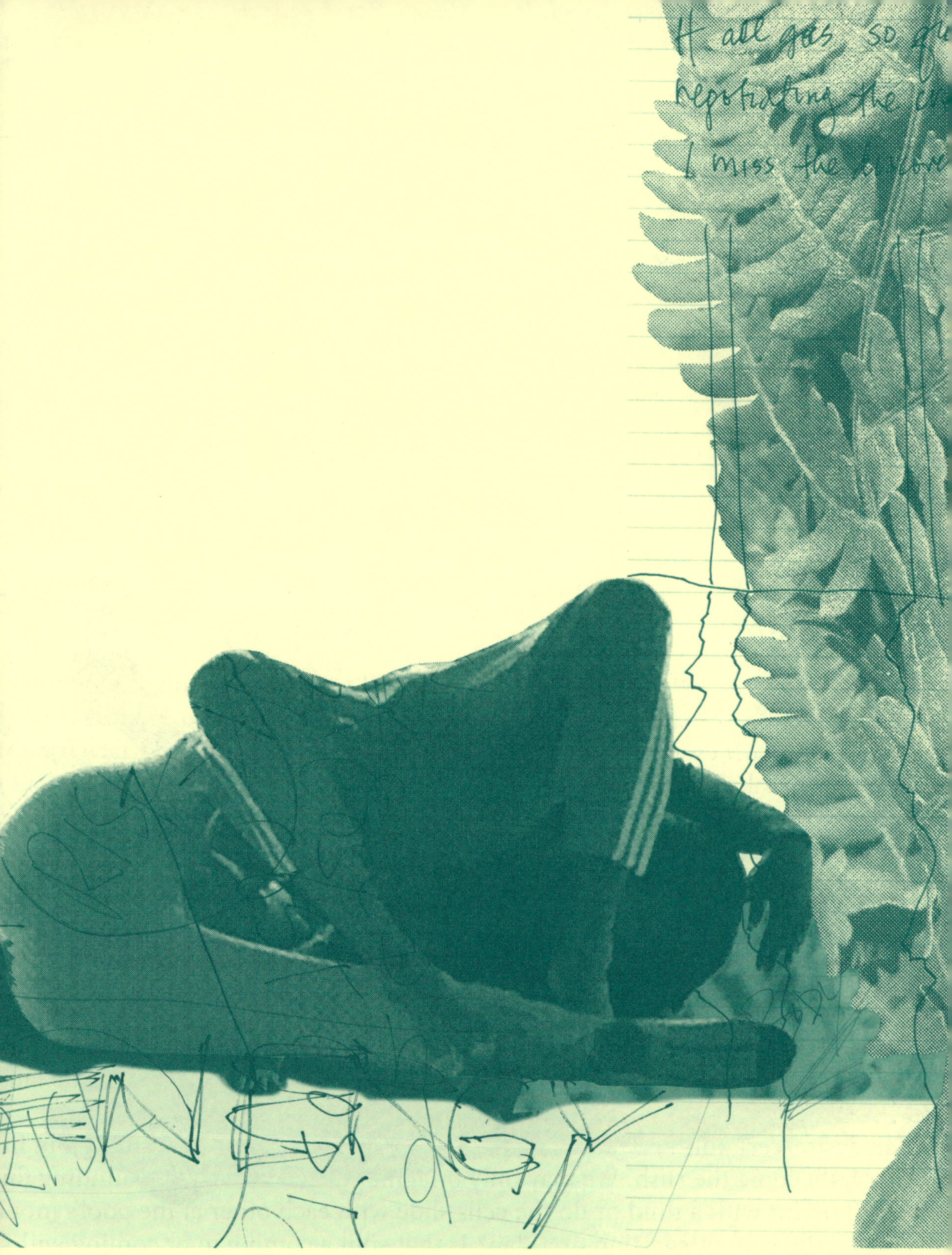

This is my favorite/familiar press

I'm the

in the picture

The body isn't merely "mine" as it turns out, as it wants things and attention. It belongs to others and all their vocabularies that fall from some other cliffs or turfs, or lands, sometimes, in somebody else's lap. It knows objects and surface friction. It knows it can take on its slippery dark interior and wear it like an old inside-out leather button-down shirt—worn so many times that finally it feels nearly transparent. At one point fingers touch tail and pubic bone, bones are identified through one's own touch—a touch trained to move beyond skin and fluids (the rechargeability and emotionality of these ease) to make way for haptic surges, nerve endings, trailings. (They have been teaching us this all along. Along a path of resistances, this generation plunders along.) The body longs for the haunt of one's attention, something beyond itself. Too, there is the feeling of walking along a many-miles-high bridge. On it, just a few feet a[illegible] waterfall po[illegible] its weight into a pool far below you. Some of its spray [illegible] you [illegible] fall down into the fray. Its fero[illegible]empts. Wh[illegible]inty?) of accidentally jumpi[illegible] with [illegible] the rush. We may only imagi[illegible]id hit with a thud or do the cells slide [illegible] swallow an integration or a slap? [illegible]at howling, propulsive, vibrational [illegible] come the current. It starts differently [illegible]at is built into the word and what it wants [illegible], that too-deep "inner" and achy-protruding [illegible] the femur bone has our attention. It [illegible] as it [illegible] as a stabilizer. It is actually [illegible] to run. Behind multiple [illegible] identify [illegible] its long history [illegible]osses, [illegible] in the effo[illegible] stand. [illegible] much [illegible] an ass [illegible] others, [illegible] the front. [illegible] the same [illegible]moving standstill. [illegible]ves from whe[illegible] blends [illegible]sterior, or from ventral to coronal, or where top falls towards a bottom.

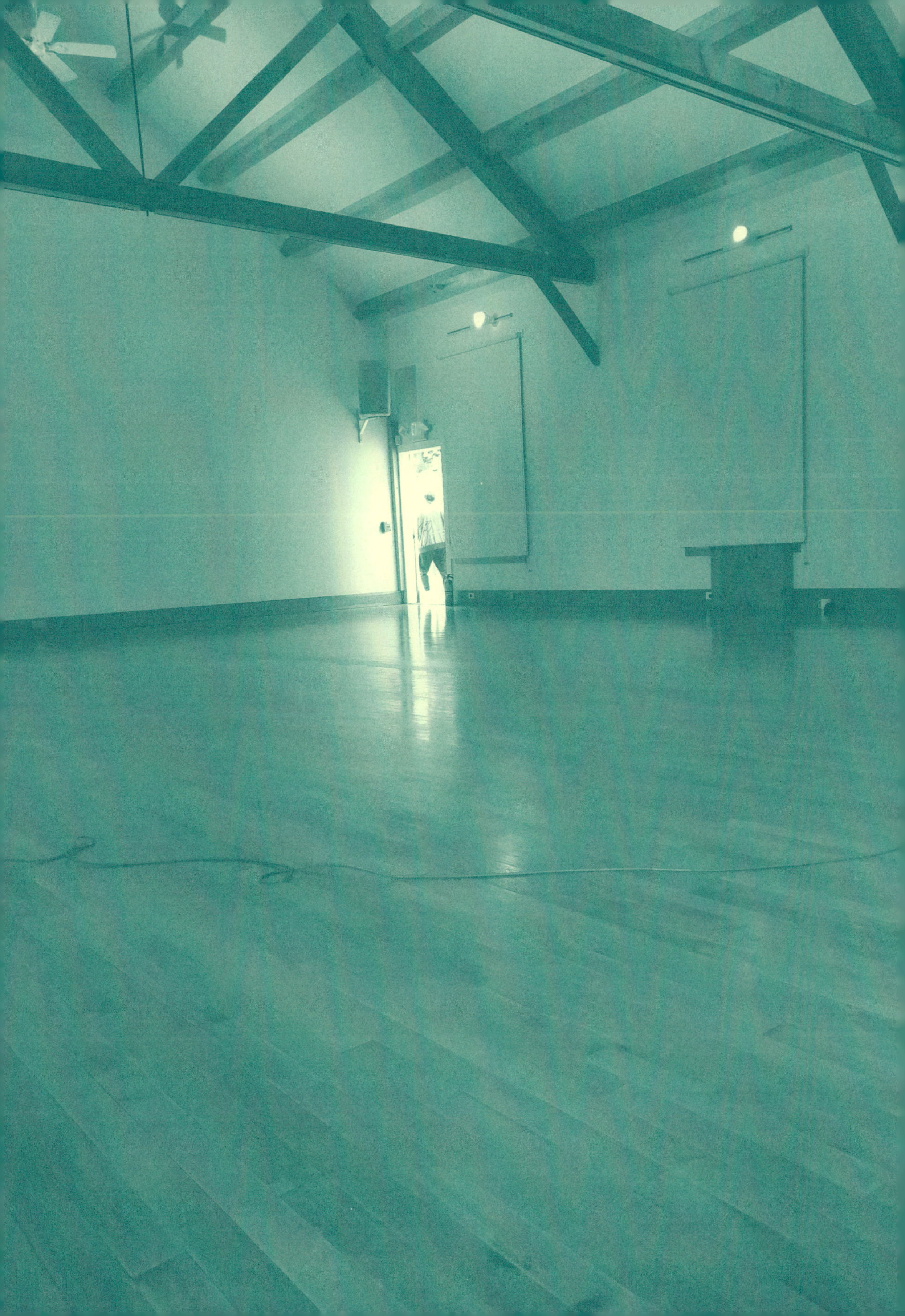

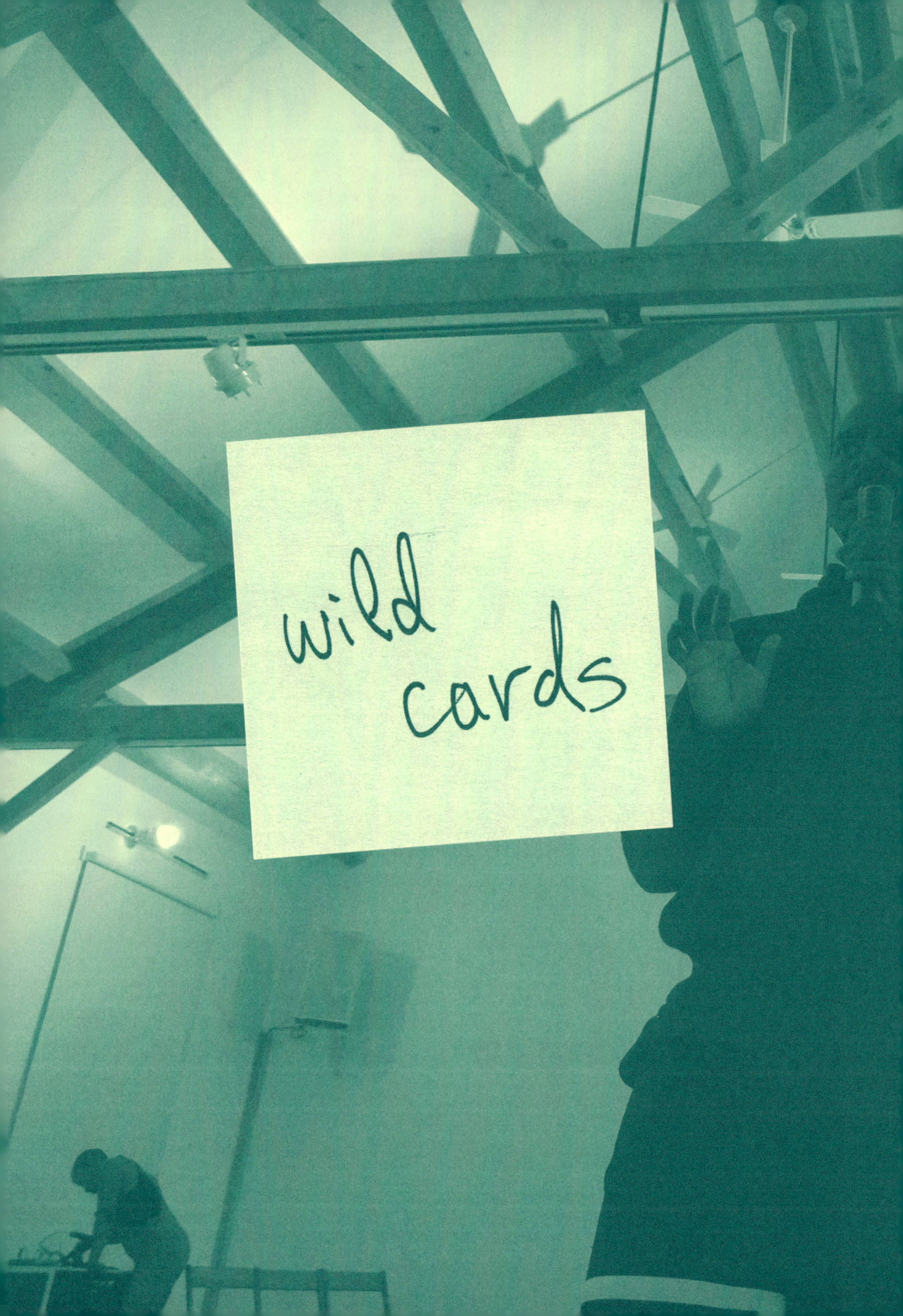
wild
cards

To introduce a wild card into a card game, or an improvisation activity, is to add an extra element of the unknown—willingly. It helps us to not get stuck, to not assume we know what will happen next. It is making a game more like life, which increasingly feels stacked with more wild cards than anything else. We entered this project with questions and a desire to be pushed into new ways of thinking about writing and performance. The process of selecting artists was a wild-carding in itself—where we would go depended on who we were. Each of us came in holding our own wild cards that life had happened to throw our way that week, that month, that year. The Jaime, the Tara, the Mlondi, the Julie, the David, the Mariana, and the Taka that appeared that week were contingent on the time and circumstances we found ourselves in. The wild cards shaped us more than anything. And then all of our wild cards bouncing off, reflecting, attracting, repelling, congealing, multiplying—sometimes in ways that were visible, usually not. We tried to care for each other and ourselves, to move through each day open to amending, to making amends. We were cognizant of our placement(s) within a stacked deck. This publication, a year later, arises in another "moment," another point in history, where wild cards have combined in a particular way within our collective deck to produce a previously unthought-of trajectory. There will always be wild cards, but there are only certain times in which the possibility of a whole new arrangement feels possible. We are in the thick of the unknown, but we sense a shadow life taking form around, above, below us, where we are in communion, where we are safe, where we are wild and free.

JSC
JULY 8, 2020

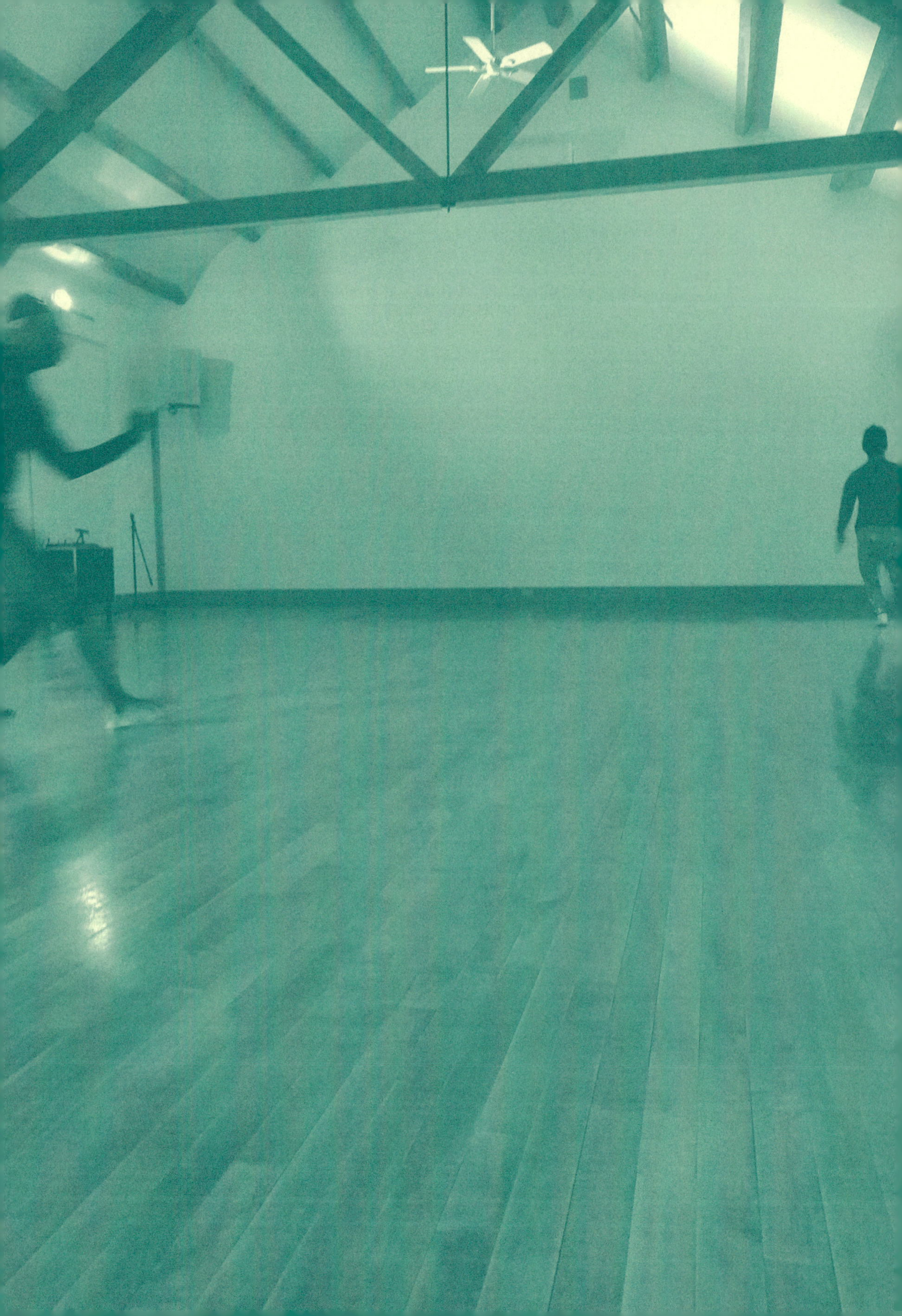

mapping the occasion

David Thomson

as I write this introduction, I am
contemplating what the future will hold
with millions of bodies clamoring for change
after months of lockdown
mouths shielded
breath abated

George Floyd broke the floodgates
and we cried out
in a torrent of pain and refusal
the rupture
the watershed
the bursting of the dam
a surging choreography
in time and space

a year ago we gathered
divining dialogues
marking time
in body and on page

here is a memory
an edited space
our voices mapped out
in prescient streams

the mundane
the poetic
the enigmatic
the manifesto

this is a score
a relational choreography
of time and space
to travel across
to wander within
a multivoiced terrain
of entangled pathways
and resonant bridges
to catalyze, soothe, and ponder

make your own meaning
find your own space

STUDIO LOFT

STUDIO

FIREPIT

LIVING ROOM 1

LIVING ROOM 2

PORCH

GARDEN

place of rest
place of unknowing (JSC, p. 120)

STUDIO LOFT

It's when someone asks you
to pause (JSC, p. 153)

i hear a plane passing
(JSC, p. 153)

how is your heart (JSC, p. 153)

STUDIO

You can strengthen the tender spots without making them become tough (JSC, p. 115)

FIREPIT

pressure from our yin places (JSC, p. 115)

LIVING ROOM 1

LIVING ROOM 2

makes me think of the spatialization of time (JSC, p. 139)

PORCH

this is what i see
this is where i am
a part in a whole
a whole in a part (JSC, p. 169)

GARDEN

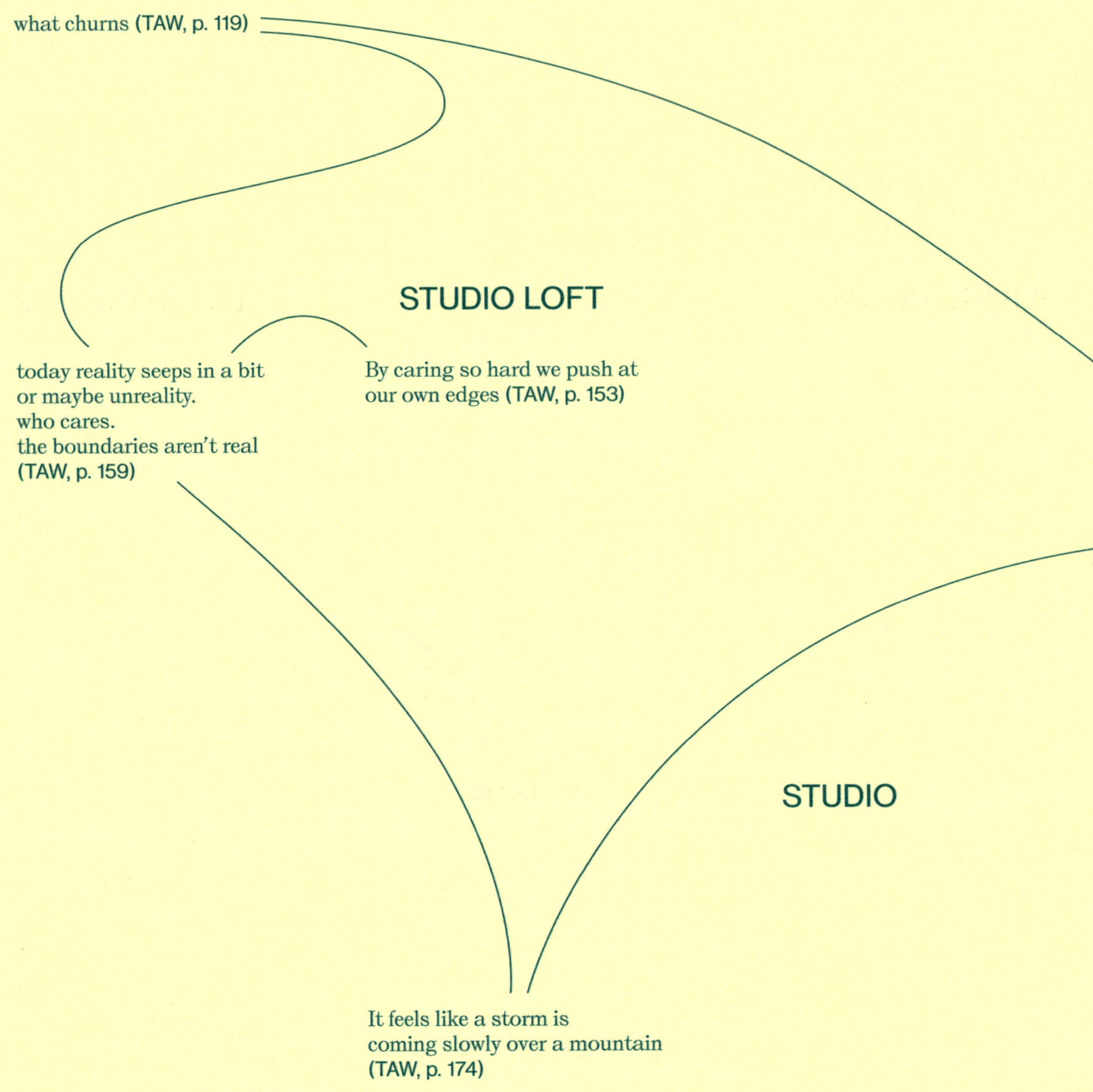
what churns (TAW, p. 119)
STUDIO LOFT
today reality seeps in a bit
or maybe unreality.
who cares.
the boundaries aren't real
(TAW, p. 159)
By caring so hard we push at
our own edges (TAW, p. 153)
STUDIO
It feels like a storm is
coming slowly over a mountain
(TAW, p. 174)

FIREPIT

LIVING ROOM 1

nonsense is the best remedy for anxiety (TAW, p. 135)

trying to trace a different or more wholistic geography for how people moved themselves (TAW, p. 133)

Maybe today there's a way of removing the obstinate feeling of being overcome by an absent thing, intangible and lingering (TAW, p. 139)

LIVING ROOM 2

What's left?
Nothing but the way a body falls into a chair with such conviction in its own familiar shape (TAW, p. 139)

PORCH

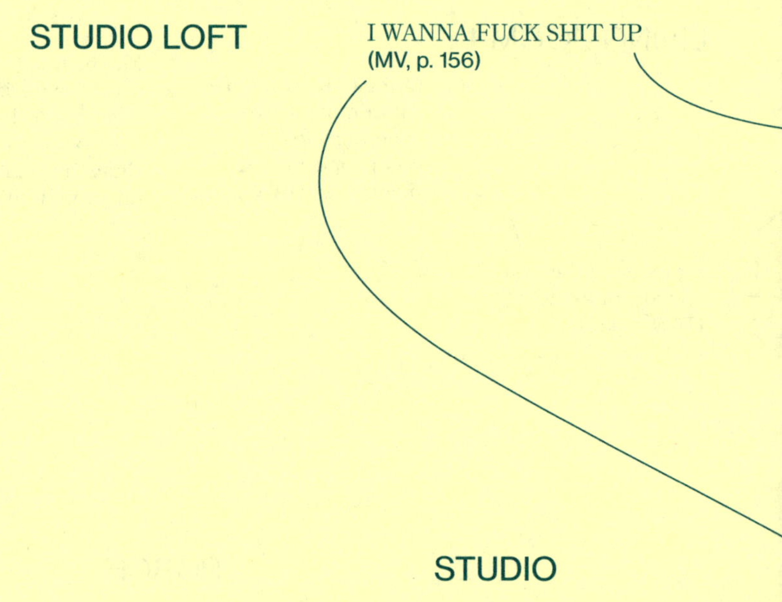
STUDIO LOFT
I WANNA FUCK SHIT UP
(MV, p. 156)
STUDIO

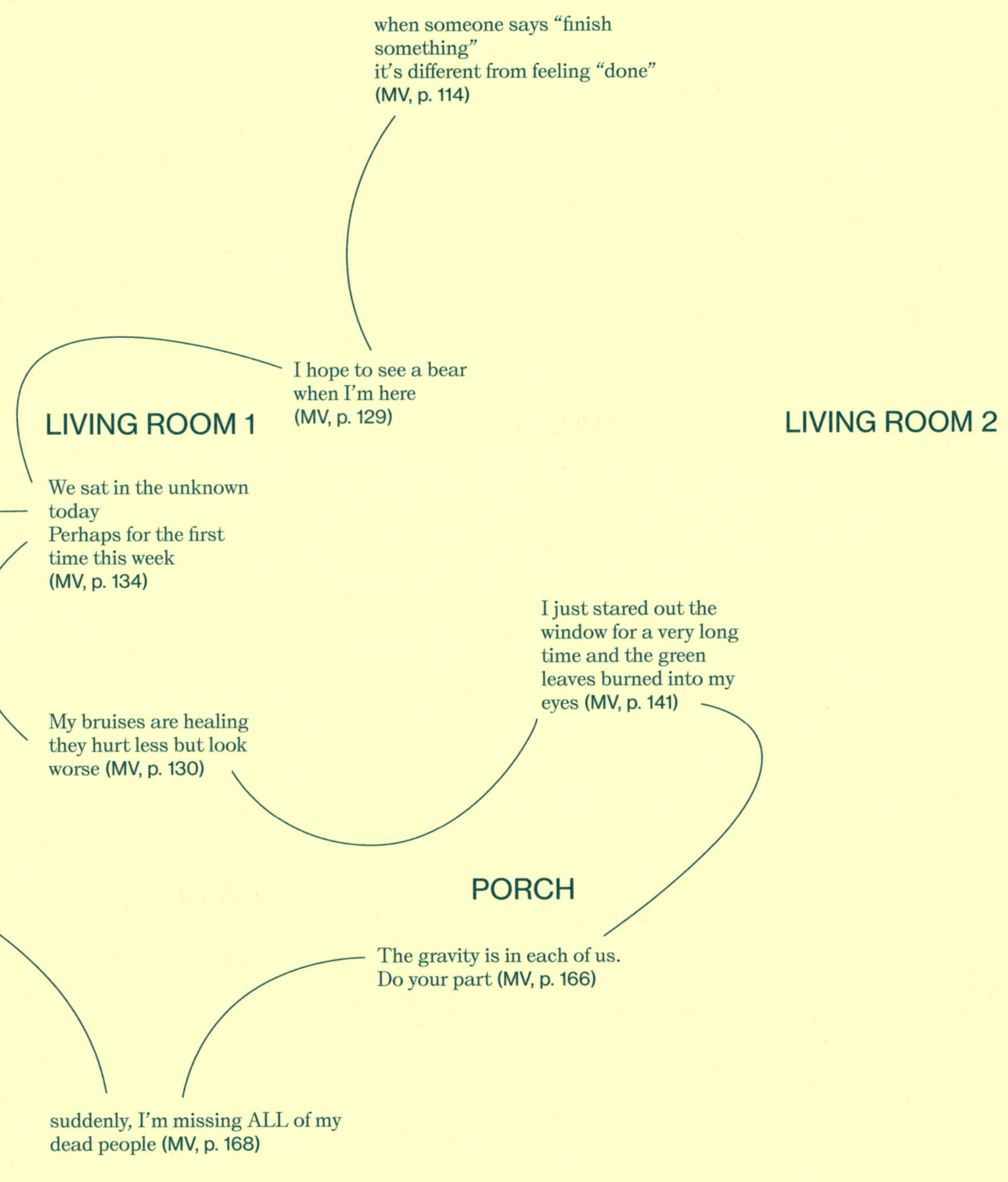
FIREPIT
when someone says "finish
something"
it's different from feeling "done"
(MV, p. 114)
I hope to see a bear
when I'm here
(MV, p. 129)
LIVING ROOM 1
LIVING ROOM 2
We sat in the unknown
today
Perhaps for the first
time this week
(MV, p. 134)
I just stared out the
window for a very long
time and the green
leaves burned into my
eyes (MV, p. 141)
My bruises are healing
they hurt less but look
worse (MV, p. 130)
PORCH
The gravity is in each of us.
Do your part (MV, p. 166)
suddenly, I'm missing ALL of my
dead people (MV, p. 168)

Playing
I keep hearing this word.
Playing (TY, p. 118)

STUDIO LOFT

STUDIO

the heat that I felt from the body of others (TY, p. 173)

Something that relies on opacity
Something that is abstract
Something that is mystical
(TY, p. 178)

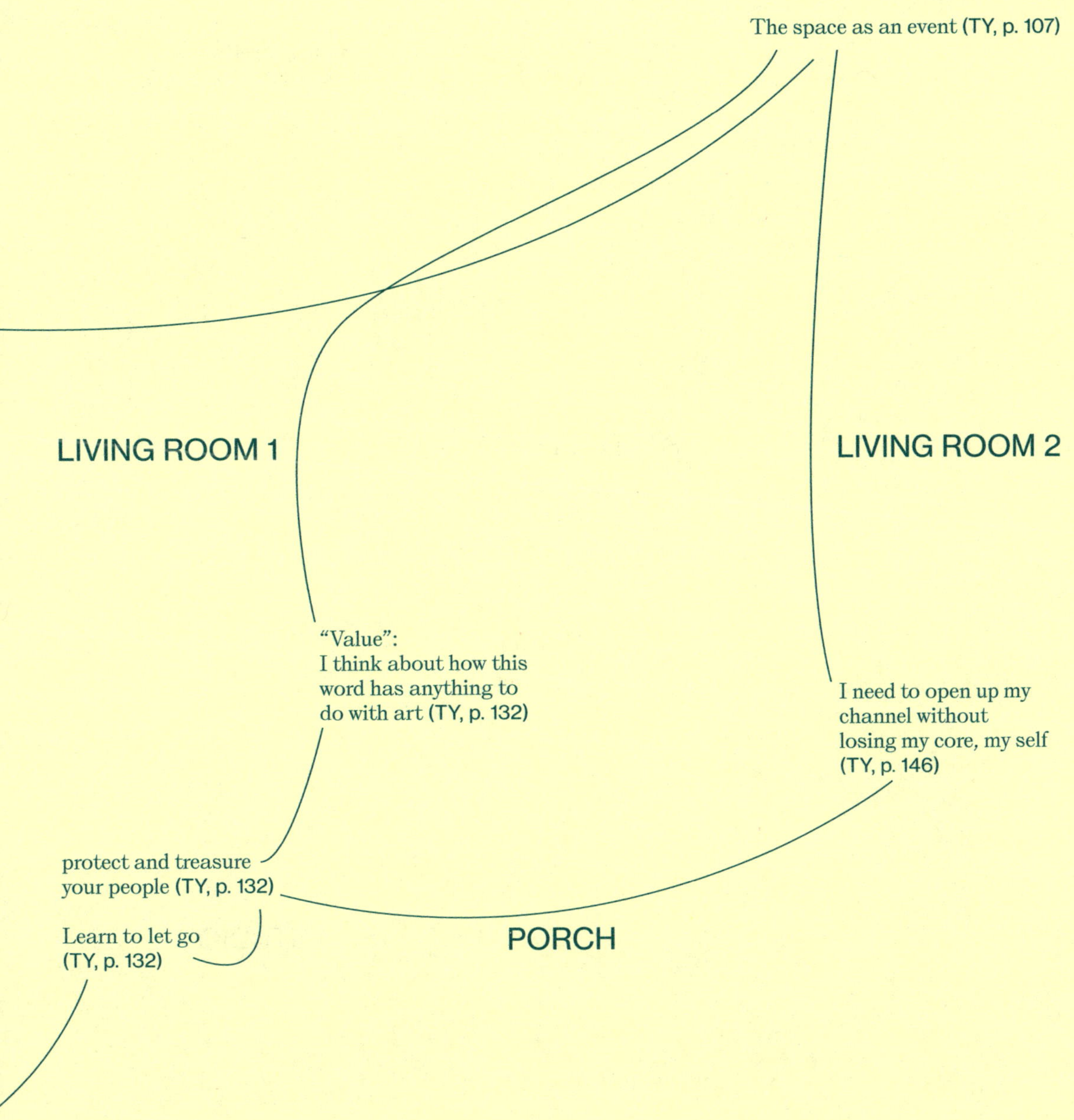
FIREPIT
The space as an event (TY, p. 107)
LIVING ROOM 1
LIVING ROOM 2
"Value":
I think about how this
word has anything to
do with art (TY, p. 132)
I need to open up my
channel without
losing my core, my self
(TY, p. 146)
protect and treasure
your people (TY, p. 132)
Learn to let go
(TY, p. 132)
PORCH

Listening itself would
be the dance (MZ, p. 126)

STUDIO LOFT

STUDIO

It is every sonic vibration
it is every earth shake
it is every bead of sweat
(MZ, p. 171)

FIREPIT

The body
The cogito
The body
The map we mistook for the territory
The body
The violence of metaphor
(MZ, p. 111)

Hell No Manifesto
(MZ, p. 57)

The chorus is still choking (MZ, p. 140)

LIVING ROOM 1

LIVING ROOM 2

Free not as a destiny, but perhaps as a different starting point
(MZ, p. 129)

PORCH

The Lord is...
the law
the testimony
the unseen
the ghost
the guilty
the evidence
the judged
the testimony
the police
the cathedral
the panopticon
the prison
my shepherd (MZ, p. 167)

The complaint is what we need
(MZ, p. 55)

The complaint is creativity, is wanting more, is knowledge that more is deserved (MZ, p. 55)

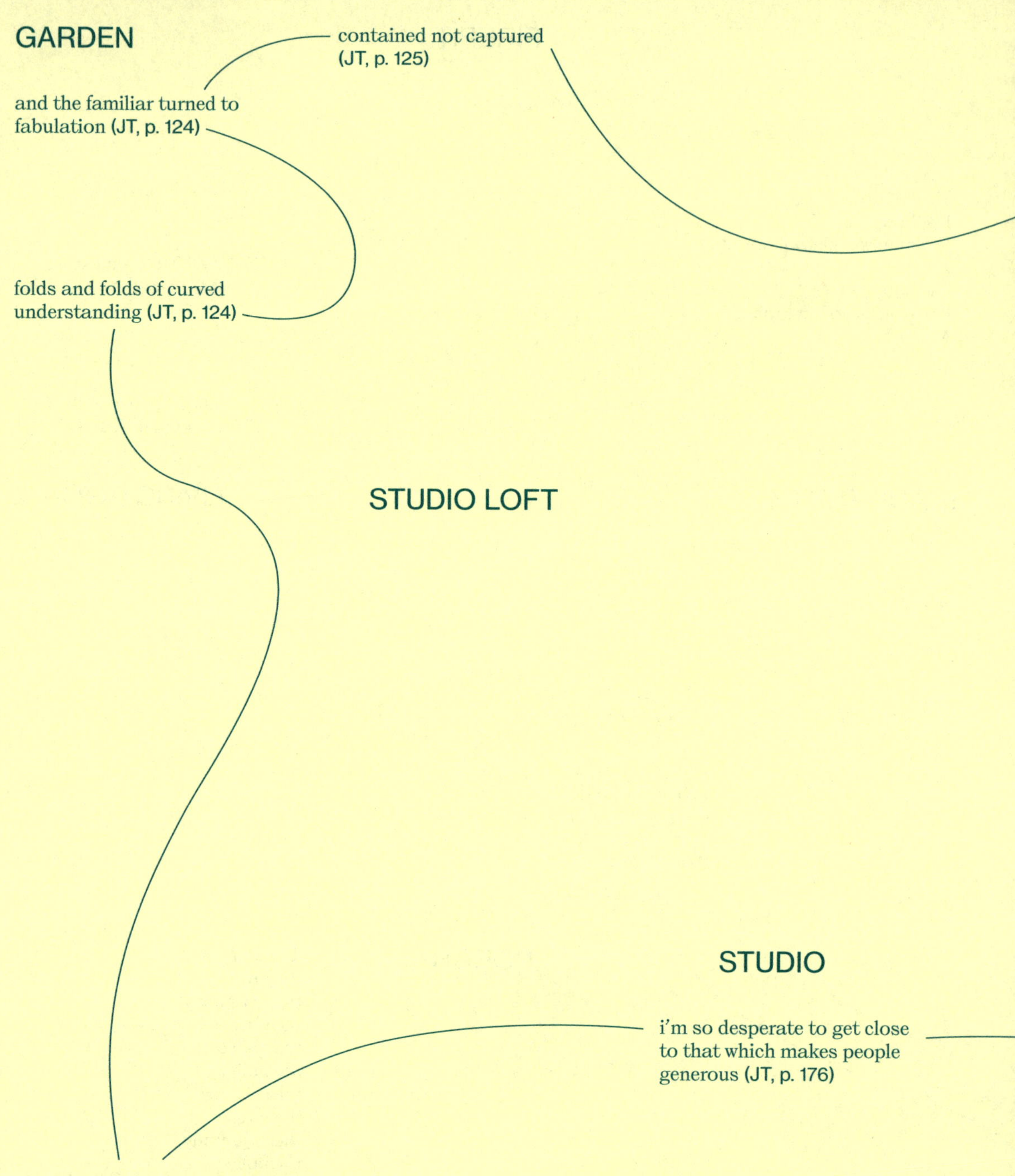
GARDEN
contained not captured
(JT, p. 125)
and the familiar turned to
fabulation (JT, p. 124)
folds and folds of curved
understanding (JT, p. 124)
STUDIO LOFT
STUDIO
i'm so desperate to get close
to that which makes people
generous (JT, p. 176)
My voice is trembling with what I
cannot touch inside of (JT, p. 176)

FIREPIT

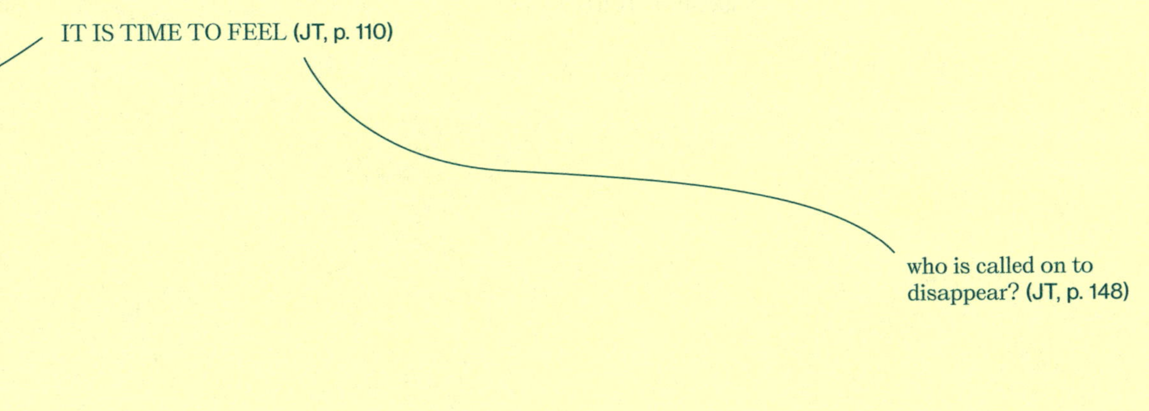

LIVING ROOM 1

LIVING ROOM 2

PORCH

return
reiterate
refuse
refine
redact (JT, p. 164)

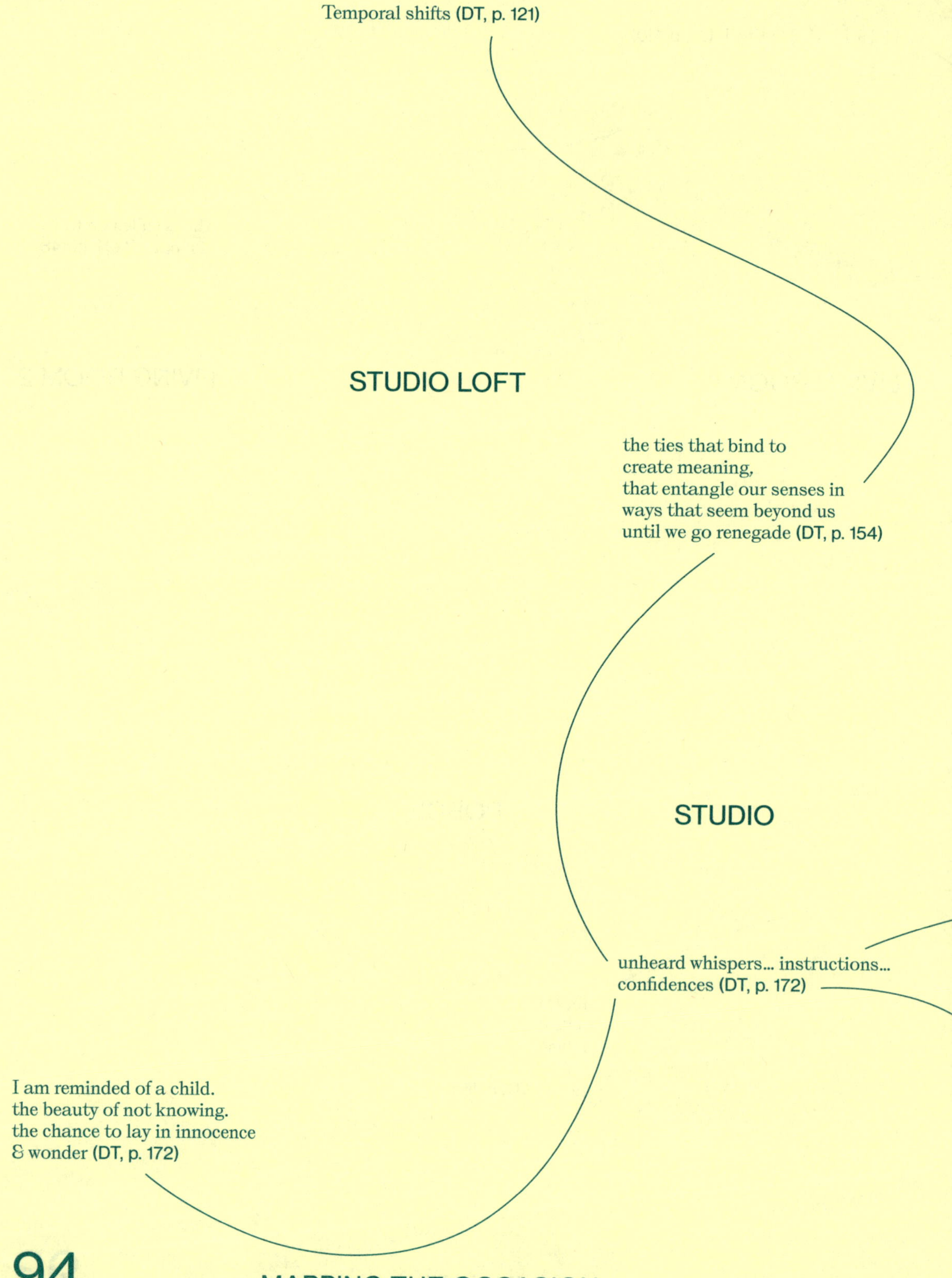
Temporal shifts (DT, p. 121)
STUDIO LOFT
the ties that bind to
create meaning,
that entangle our senses in
ways that seem beyond us
until we go renegade (DT, p. 154)
STUDIO
unheard whispers... instructions...
confidences (DT, p. 172)
I am reminded of a child.
the beauty of not knowing.
the chance to lay in innocence
& wonder (DT, p. 172)

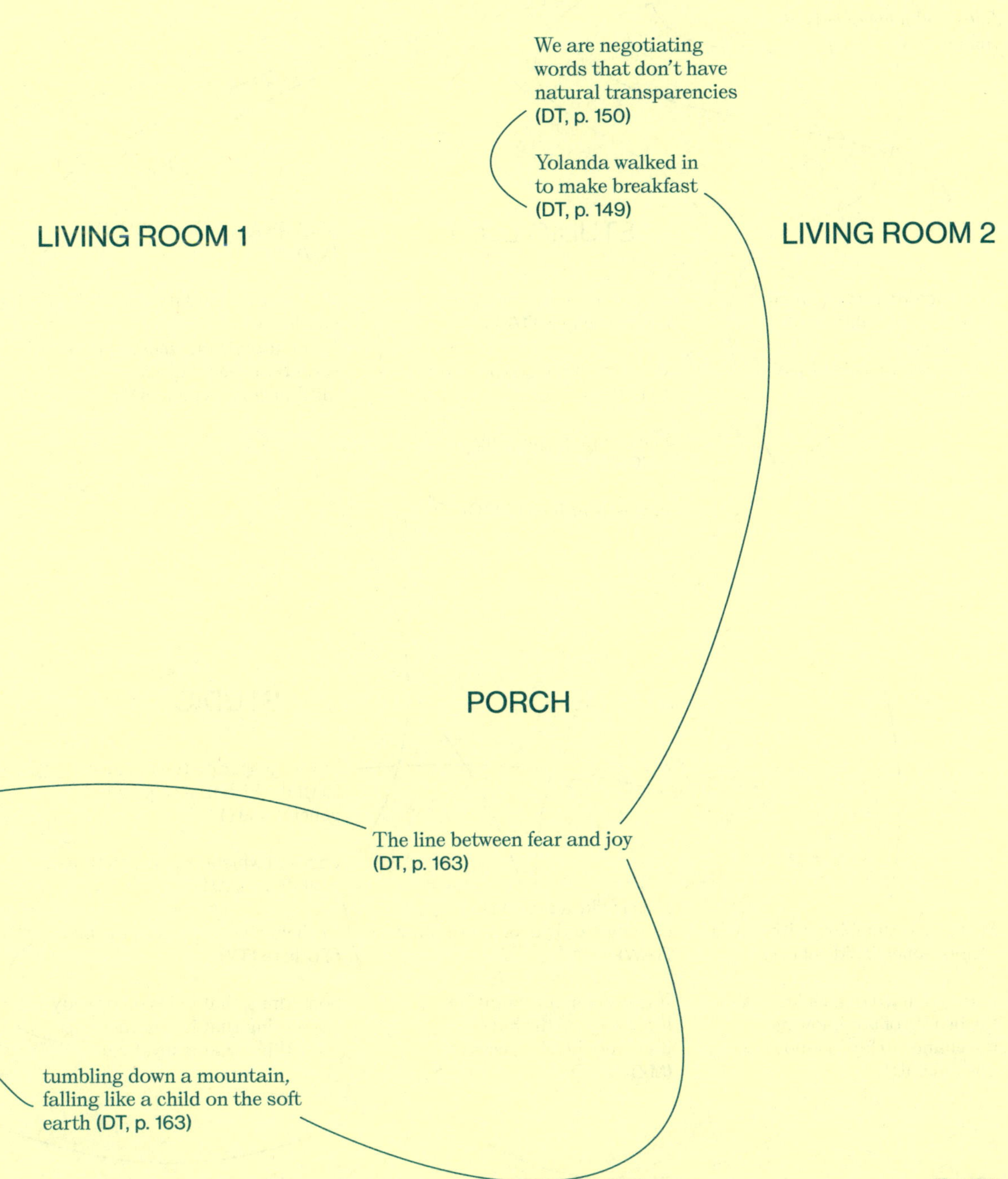
FIREPIT
We are negotiating words that don't have natural transparencies (DT, p. 150)
Yolanda walked in to make breakfast (DT, p. 149)
LIVING ROOM 1
LIVING ROOM 2
PORCH
The line between fear and joy (DT, p. 163)
tumbling down a mountain, falling like a child on the soft earth (DT, p. 163)

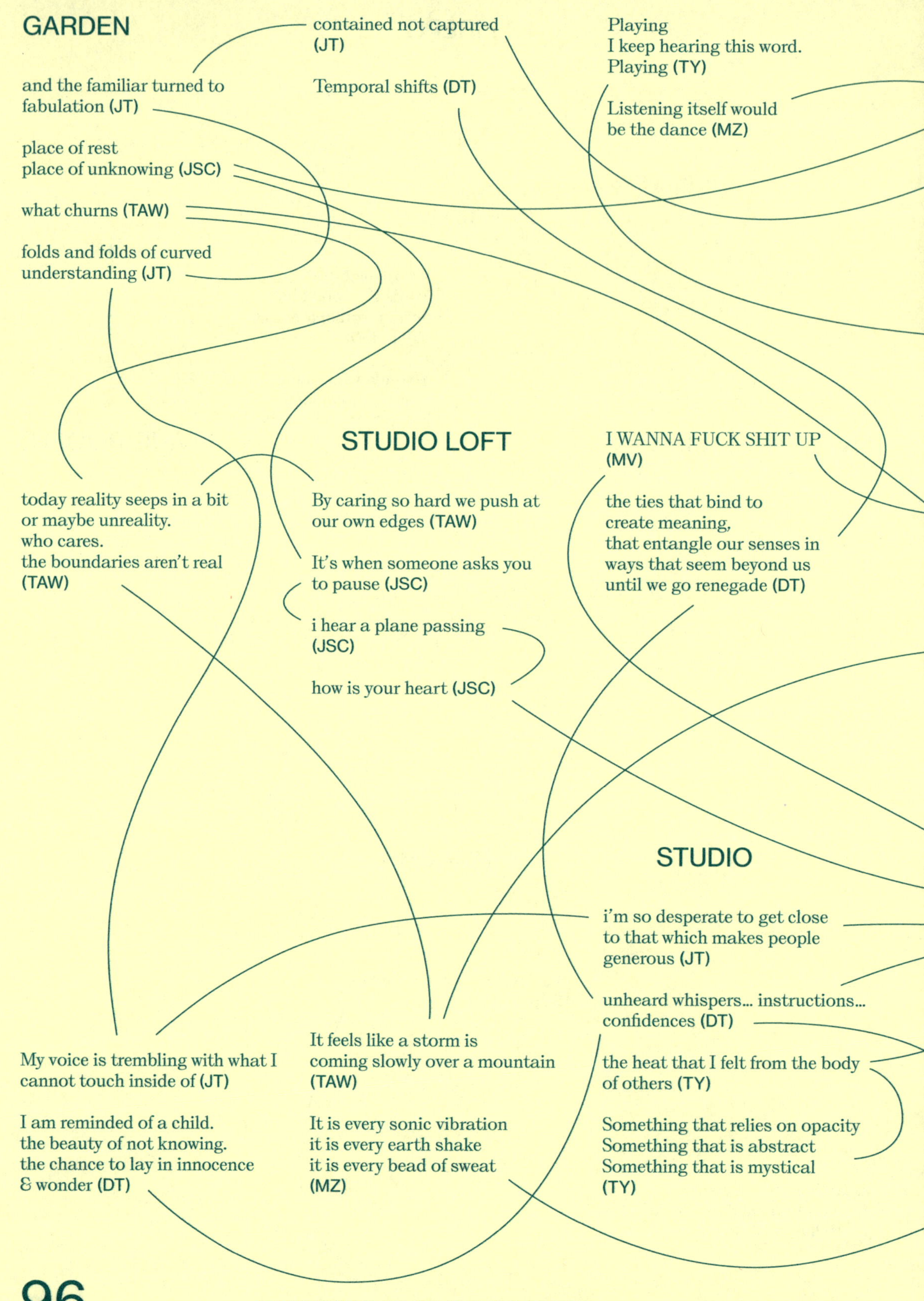
GARDEN
contained not captured (JT)
Playing
I keep hearing this word.
Playing (TY)
and the familiar turned to fabulation (JT)
Temporal shifts (DT)
Listening itself would be the dance (MZ)
place of rest
place of unknowing (JSC)
what churns (TAW)
folds and folds of curved understanding (JT)
STUDIO LOFT
I WANNA FUCK SHIT UP (MV)
today reality seeps in a bit
or maybe unreality.
who cares.
the boundaries aren't real (TAW)
By caring so hard we push at our own edges (TAW)
the ties that bind to
create meaning,
that entangle our senses in
ways that seem beyond us
until we go renegade (DT)
It's when someone asks you to pause (JSC)
i hear a plane passing (JSC)
how is your heart (JSC)
STUDIO
i'm so desperate to get close
to that which makes people
generous (JT)
unheard whispers... instructions...
confidences (DT)
It feels like a storm is
coming slowly over a mountain
(TAW)
My voice is trembling with what I
cannot touch inside of (JT)
the heat that I felt from the body
of others (TY)
I am reminded of a child.
the beauty of not knowing.
the chance to lay in innocence
& wonder (DT)
It is every sonic vibration
it is every earth shake
it is every bead of sweat
(MZ)
Something that relies on opacity
Something that is abstract
Something that is mystical
(TY)

FIREPIT

You can strengthen the tender spots without making them become tough (JSC)

IT IS TIME TO FEEL (JT)

The body
The cogito
The body
The map we mistook for the territory
The body
The violence of metaphor
(MZ)

when someone says "finish something"
it's different from feeling "done"
(MV)

pressure from our yin places
(JSC)

The space as an event (TY)

Hell No Manifesto
(MZ)

who is called on to disappear? (JT)

The chorus is still choking (MZ)

We are negotiating words that don't have natural transparencies
(DT)

Yolanda walked in to make breakfast
(DT)

I hope to see a bear when I'm here
(MV)

LIVING ROOM 1

We sat in the unknown today
Perhaps for the first time this week
(MV)

nonsense is the best remedy for anxiety
(TAW)

My bruises are healing they hurt less but look worse (MV)

protect and treasure your people (TY)

Learn to let go
(TY)

trying to trace a different or more wholistic geography for how people moved themselves (TAW)

"Value":
I think about how this word has anything to do with art (TY)

Free not as a destiny, but perhaps as a different starting point
(MZ)

Maybe today there's a way of removing the obstinate feeling of being overcome by an absent thing, intangible and lingering (TAW)

I just stared out the window for a very long time and the green leaves burned into my eyes (MV)

makes me think of the spatialization of time
(JSC)

LIVING ROOM 2

What's left?
Nothing but the way a body falls into a chair with such conviction in its own familiar shape
(TAW)

I need to open up my channel without losing my core, my self
(TY)

PORCH

The gravity is in each of us.
Do your part (MV)

The line between fear and joy
(DT)

return
reiterate
refuse
refine
redact (JT)

The complaint is creativity, is wanting more, is knowledge that more is deserved (MZ)

suddenly, I'm missing ALL of my dead people (MV)

The complaint is what we need
(MZ)

tumbling down a mountain, falling like a child on the soft earth (DT)

The Lord is...
the law
the testimony
the unseen
the ghost
the guilty
the evidence
the judged
the testimony
the police
the cathedral
the panopticon
the prison
my shepherd (MZ)

this is what i see
this is where i am
a part in a whole
a whole in a part (JSC)

and the familiar turned to fabulation

place of rest
place of unknowing

what churns

folds and folds of curved understanding

contained not captured

Temporal shifts

Playing
I keep hearing this word.
Playing

Listening itself would be the dance

I WANNA FUCK SHIT UP

today reality seeps in a bit
or maybe unreality.
who cares.
the boundaries aren't real

By caring so hard we push at our own edges

It's when someone asks you to pause

i hear a plane passing

how is your heart

the ties that bind to
create meaning,
that entangle our senses in
ways that seem beyond us
until we go renegade

i'm so desperate to get close to that which makes people generous

unheard whispers... instructions... confidences

My voice is trembling with what I cannot touch inside of

I am reminded of a child.
the beauty of not knowing.
the chance to lay in innocence
& wonder

It feels like a storm is coming slowly over a mountain

It is every sonic vibration
it is every earth shake
it is every bead of sweat

the heat that I felt from the body of others

Something that relies on opacity
Something that is abstract
Something that is mystical

You can strengthen the tender spots without making them become tough

IT IS TIME TO FEEL

The body
The cogito
The body
The map we mistook for the territory
The body
The violence of metaphor

We sat in the unknown today
Perhaps for the first time this week

nonsense is the best remedy for anxiety

My bruises are healing they hurt less but look worse

protect and treasure your people

Learn to let go

suddenly, I'm missing ALL of my dead people

The complaint is what we need

tumbling down a mountain, falling like a child on the soft earth

when someone says "finish something"
it's different from feeling "done"

I hope to see a bear when I'm here

trying to trace a different or more wholistic geography for how people moved themselves

"Value":
I think about how this word has anything to do with art

Free not as a destiny, but perhaps as a different starting point

The gravity is in each of us.
Do your part

The line between fear and joy

return
reiterate
refuse
refine
redact

The complaint is creativity, is wanting more, is knowledge that more is deserved

We are negotiating words that don't have natural transparencies

Yolanda walked in to make breakfast

Maybe today there's a way of removing the obstinate feeling of being overcome by an absent thing, intangible and lingering

I just stared out the window for a very long time and the green leaves burned into my eyes

makes me think of the spatialization of time

pressure from our yin places

The space as an event

Hell No Manifesto

who is called on to disappear?

The chorus is still choking

What's left?
Nothing but the way a body falls into a chair with such conviction in its own familiar shape

I need to open up my channel without losing my core, my self

The Lord is...
the law
the testimony
the unseen
the ghost
the guilty
the evidence
the judged
the testimony
the police
the cathedral
the panopticon
the prison
my shepherd

this is what i see
this is where i am
a part in a whole
a whole in a part

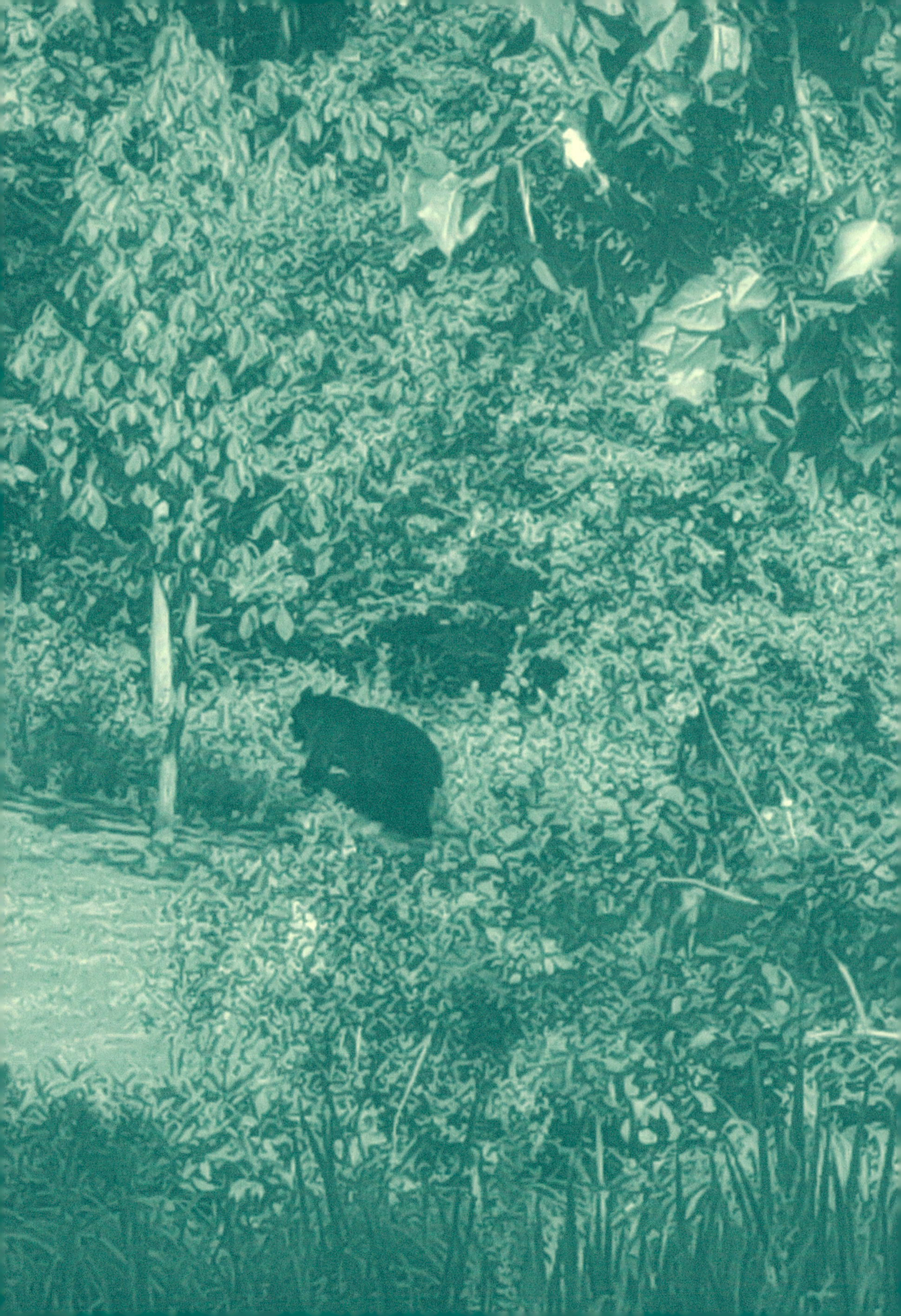

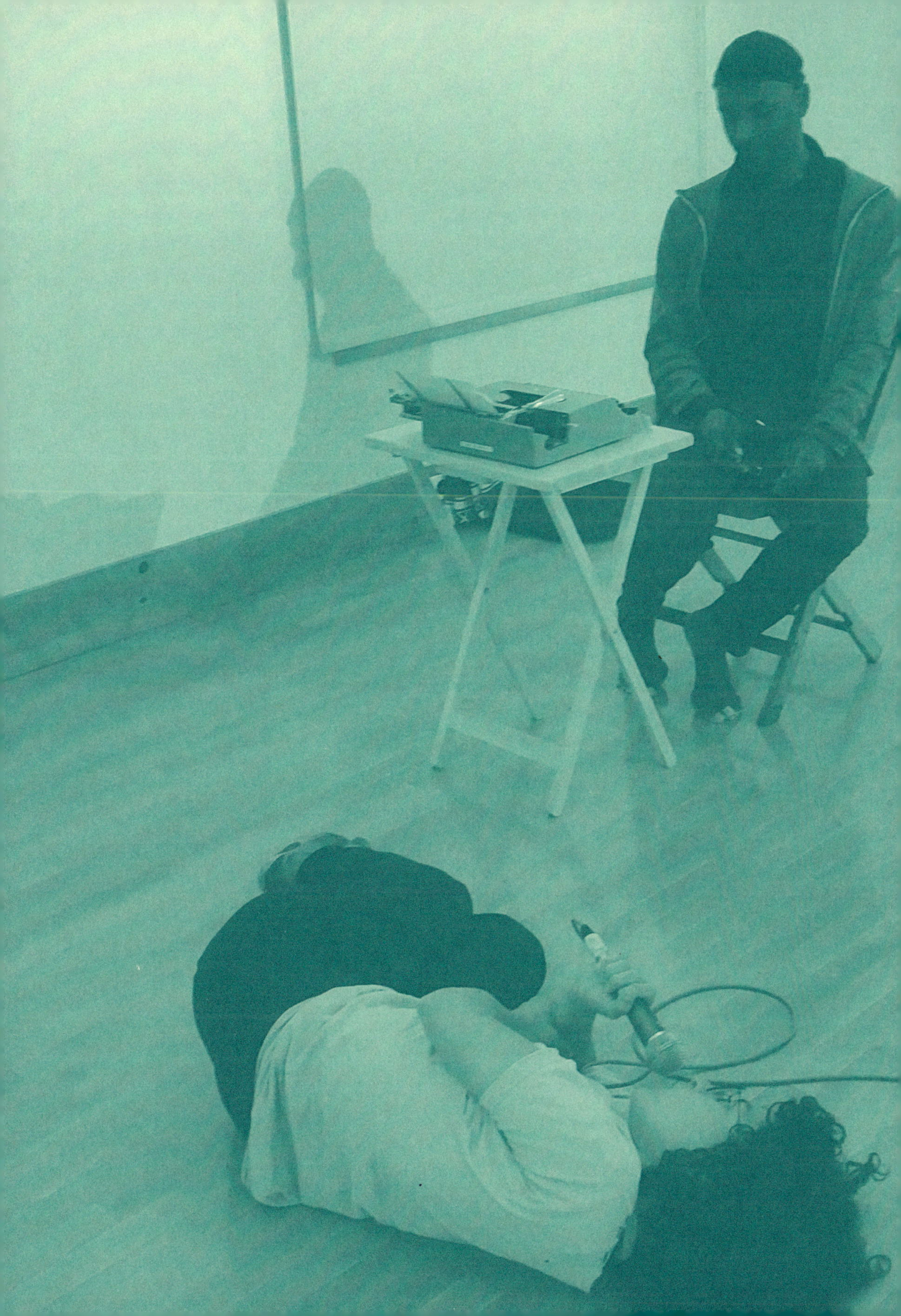

typewriter
+
body mic

There are multiple ways of marking an occasion. Sometimes the marking is folded up inside the occasion itself, allowed to drift from the impulse to the archive, to document in now-time for another time. The evidence left by the thing that happened is part of the thing that happened. Inside the studio, you type as many words as you can catch as they are whispered in your ear by another performer who reads from a notebook entry someone else wrote two days before on the porch. The occasion stretches taut and wide from the handwritten pages to the typewritten ones, buoyed up in between by a body or two, a voice keeping up with its own words like a game of telephone, and of *time.* Inside the studio, you round your mouth above the metal of the microphone in your eagerness to make your whispers reach beyond your body, reading from a notebook entry someone else wrote while sitting in the garden just before they picked some green onions for lunch. Inside your mouth, you mangle those words with the pickings you've made from the ones whispered in your ear by another performer, read from yet another notebook entry written on another day, this time up in the studio loft under which you now crouch in the dark, expelling a mesh of words and sounds: a spell for transmogrifying the distance between doing and marking. A year later, none of these intimacies—fingers sharing typewriter keys, mouth against ear or mic—is on its way back to us. Too much spittle and bile. Droplets too far from the body. Bodies too close together. At least the studio windows were open to circulate air. At least you each had your own bedroom for the week: a room with a new meaning now, ready to become an "isolation chamber" in the quick shudder of sudden quarantine. There are multiple ways to mark an occasion, many ways to expel words. Occasionally, they stick.

TAW
JULY 8, 2020

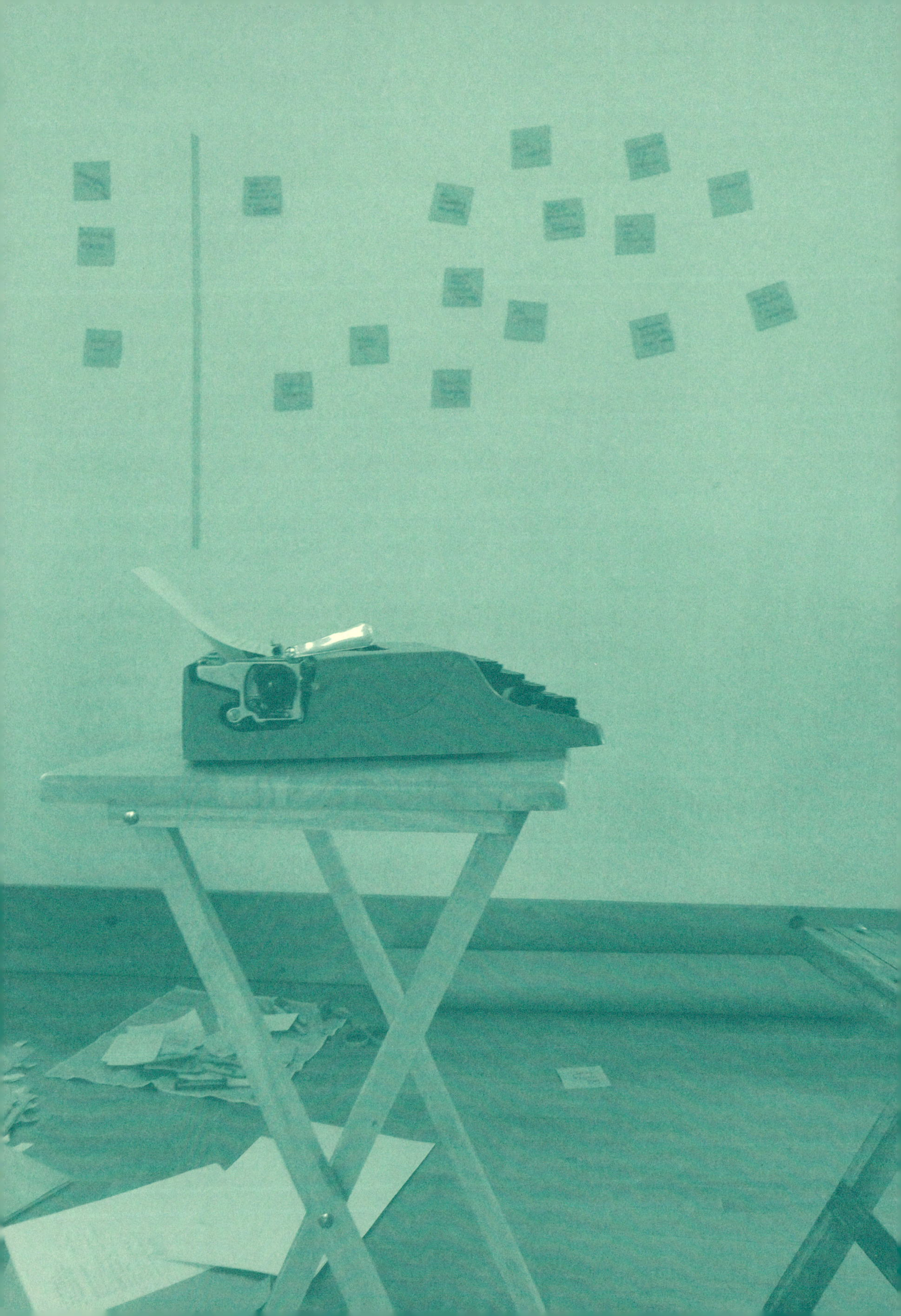

NOTEBOOKS

Selections from
June 11–16, 2019

FIREPIT

To take pure perception first. When we make the cerebral state the beginning of an action, and in no sense the condition of a perception, we place the perceived images of things outside the image of our body, and thus replace perception within the things themselves. But then, our perception being a part of things, things participate in the nature of our perception.

—181, 182

Now, if every concrete perception, however short we suppose it, is already a synthesis, made by memory, of an infinity of "pure perceptions" which succeed each other, must we not think that the heterogeneity of sensible qualities is due to their being contracted in our memory and the relative homogeneity of objective changes to the slackness of their natural tension?

—182, 183 Bergson.

This lime green color. This angular shapes. I feel the shape in my hand, legs, and my butt: the hardness of it, the temperature of it, through its shape and material. This direct and tactile perception, or maybe that's sensation.

This beautifully-taken-care-of environment. This naturally-noisy space with occasional sound of cars driving by. I see. The vast amount of visual information surrounding me; yet, it also creates, somehow effortlessly, a whole. The space as an event, a singular event.

This movement of dandelion's seed falling down to the ground. This ~~moving~~, even after the landing, moving along the concrete nudged by the wind. The ~~gr~~ gravity of it all. The insistence of reproduction, distribution (relational), and sex. Thinking and perceiving the natural, in this case, one with dandelions, reproduction reminds me how vastly profound, emotionally-charged, time-numbing sex can be, for us, for us humans.

This lighting fixture. This string-tied round light bulbs hanging along the porch. Almost unnecessary. however, it adds more context: morning as a ~~[illegible]~~ remainder of night: waste of electronic energy (but it's only a waste when you only ~~thin~~ perceive it as a mere functional objects. But maybe you/I should?): human convenience, in style.

This cool air/breeze. This air harmonized with the sound of young tree leaves in constant frixion. As pleasant as it is, I was notified/informed that it'll be rainy tomorrow. Weather forecast. Future-oriented invention. Preparedness. Planning. The sense of ease that is associated with this "planning." A sense of knowing where/what/how. Being in a present, only in a present, is not the most comforting space because our body/our physical body, never stops in time.

Taka. 10am 6/12/19

David made tapes and he wrote long monologues ~~of~~ about ~~people~~ → these ~~people were told~~ these monologues to David and David recorded them ~~in~~ from memory into writing.

From memory into writing.
I never met David but when I read about him or read his writing I feel like I know him and when I return to his writing I remember how familiar he feels to me. Like a sibling. I suppose that's the opposite feeling of "From Memory into Writing" to "From Writing into Memory"

I had my feet (my bare feet) in the grass today. This was the first time for them this year. I think I'm also wearing my first shorts of the year.

The fire pit is a perfect place to be sitting today at this time. I'm right under the sun.

The David I'm writing about is David Wojnarowicz. The tapes book

called "the weight of the Earth."
Ethan just arrived with some milk, some charcoal and other provisions that I cannot identify.
When I look to the right, the mountains look like this:

by: MV's 6-12-19, 2pm

my body near mountain
@ 615pm
6/12/19
JT

immigrating between places
david – our friend, my friend, my friend's boyfriend, my boyfriends lover, our bandmate they'd say. i'll never forget the noise that was his body, of course his deep pressurized voice. doors close. like epochs.
what i can offer is another way to generation. She says that anyway.
need more time. i cannot in words dive. They took me and traced for me the inside the shape and effort commitments to each other perhaps instead of fear there's something else. I keep saying that and and. for bodies to emerge w/on/with the other

→ FUCK THIS WORD. Look what happens when words fail

there were GENERATIONS OF MOVEMENT
INCLUDING MINE / OURS —

SO SKINNY
SO LOST

but alas ~~MOM~~ MV prepared the space for me, allowing me to be the person to come. to be the reader so ready to know what / who

DAVID w/ SOME TAPES

was. small sounds keep escaping like gasp. gasp. the small world of cartoon. gasp. The action of a kind of only-to-oneself horror.

IT IS TIME TO FEEL. RIGOR KNOWS ~~NO OTHER~~ ~~SOME~~ ~~WORKS OUT~~ BOUNDS.

YIN PARTS.
SO MANY YIN PARTS
SHOWING. NO NEED TO "SHOW THEM"

~ SING IT BACK. ~

WE GET MESSED UP. RECOMPOSURE BECOMES A PRESSURE POINT.

little deaths
migration
illness
basements
ships
deserts
fighting it. for it. from it.
then at the 10 MIN MARK.

JT 6:25pm 1/11/2019

anastasia arrived to pull things from the area to my right. like hanging upside down asking

to

be

moved.

The Body
A machine that runs on sugar
The Body
A chemical factory unmaking itself.
The Body
Not reducible to its indexicality
The Body
A privileged possession for some
The Body
The ultimate fetish of dance study
The Body
The great unknown that everyone claims to know
The Body
Like a bank account, only some have "it"
The Body
The Cogito
The Body
The Map we mistook for the territory
The Body
The violence of metaphor
The Body
The non-"I"
The Body
Corporate
The Body
"Confusing the body with evidence" (Sharpe)
The Body
"the great equalizer"
The Body
"the greatest trick of obscuring difference"
The Body
Before dissection

The Body
White
The Body
The feminized
The Body
The Law of labor
The Body
The Corpse
Decomposition
The Body
Flesh of my flesh
The Soil
The Body
Adam's apple
The Body
Tabula Rasa
The Body
The Virtual
~~The~~ Chimera
The flower
Deflower
The Signification of the Phallus
Amputation
Miracle
Mirage
Striptease
Pus!
Pulse!
Sweat
Wet
Sentient
Delectable
Pheromones
Xenophobia
Fuck fest
And yet
I am yet
to be one
to have one.
to be haved

—Mbodi 10 am
13 June

Deserts I love:

today I sat up while others
lay on their belly while they wrote about each
other's 3 min monologue.
I stayed seated up ward with crossed leggs.
looking at the performers as they gave
words to us.

Today we will have a night session.
Today rained in the morning.
today I will go to Woodstock.
The first time I looked through a telescope at t
moon, was in my friend's Valeda and Elija's
Back Yard, They live in woodstock.
The first time I saw a bear was in MT Tremper.
What is 10 minutes?
Today, I gave a monologue about kink and
though I don't know kink, perse, I know
kink and actually might "know" it too. I
compared my not knowing of kink, to my not
knowing of Queer Theory and Star Wars. →

I don't have a middle name
David Thomson does → Hamilton
Julie Tolentino does → Maria Dominica
The things you learn when you ask.
Taka does not have a middle name.

when someone says "finish something" it's different from feeling "done"

♡ MV 6-13-19, 2pm

JSC

6/13 6:10 pm

~~A firepit is fireless~~
~~A small hatchet rests~~
~~& the crickets & the Esopus crashes~~

there is the feeling of being
in the wrong time
the firepit before dinner & after the fire burned out
too early or too late for the party
the feeling of pre-dinner
that reminds me of being a kid
when things were done for me
i'm buzzing from our collective energy
giving form to our time together

< deep breath >

i also have a middle name, Mariana
it was my grandmother's middle name too
Faye Shearn Goldsmith
I have her first name tatooed in cursive
inside of my left upper arm, a tender place
i liked when Julie told us to apply pressure
from our yin places – i didn't know what
that meant but now i do.
there is strength in the tender spots.
you can strengthen the tender spots without
making them become tough.
just more strong & sure in the tenderness.

This is transcript

recorder tape

[illegible] [illegible]

talks things about love

jokes about things

OUT FIRST TIME

I.

Thee.

When I knew that the whole point is to listen, and yet I placed myself in a very noisy place.

When we close the window as the temperature has gotten higher and higher, because we live in a 3-rd story walk-up.

When I lost my contact lens on the floor, and my father and I tried to find it for a long time because the contact lense was so expensive back then.

When I waited and waited and waited for my host mother's daughter's ex boyfriend to come pick me up to do surfing. and he never did, I was so disappointed and sad.

When I was called Hispanic in Japan because of my looks

When I got so scared of a horror movie, Final Destination, at my very first date with a girl who used to work at Payless shoes.

There.

My mind is numb, static, noise.

My body deteriorates. Image heavy.

Taka 6pm 6/14/19

GARDEN

Playing. I keep hearing this word. Playing. Maybe I just keep leaving this word in my brain/body, and it starts triggered.

I don't play so much anymore. I might be lying by saying that.

There is a sweet quality to it: inhabited, non-critical / non-editorial, embodied, no-agenda, non-capitalistic. That's right. Non-capitalistic and non-neoliberalist about this concept.

Yet, there's still an investment / commitment to its execution, which I like/enjoy.

Hyphening is something I do quite often. It means I keep re-evaluating the meaning and usage of a word and rephrase it in order to find a perfect one to match with my thinking. Which word better suit my own opinion or ideas?

Heat makes us feel lathergic. Quite often. It drains the inner energy. At the same time, it nourishes us. Vitamin-D. Energy boosting. Energy sustaining. Again, the ~~simultns~~ simultaneous duality. Separation or split of the same. Opposit attraction. Evil twin~~[illegible]~~. Coin with two faces.

Can there be coin with three faces? Four faces? Maybe, it just is a round object. Blob

Blob. Blob Blob
Blob Blob. Blob
Blob Blob Blob
Blob Blob Blob
Blob Blob
Blob Blob

David's exercise names two parties as Avater and Self. With two bodies.

I think the question is the subject self. Subjecting self. Subjected self. (that's a bit more phenomenological. Subject and object, but those two ideas are not exactly an opposit.

Blob
Blob
Blob

Taka 2pm 6/12/19

forge forget
forget
forget
evaluate & resolve
epic epoch overhaul
turn over easy dances fear
obstacle
line fly and fish
hook foot & foot & foot
& calf
over bearing
born
out side ways
return again & learn
return for the first time and release
these four things fling
is this useful? need it be?
is this beauty? beautiful? architectural?

what churns.

TAW 6.12.19
6:15 pm

[jsc 6/13 10am]

place of rest — place of unknowing

inside studio due to the (rain)

leave space [ ] for what you don't understand

david teaches us that

i use hyphens a lot, they allow
a loose alliance to exist

without forcing a particular relationship

my left hand palms a mug of hot tea and my right is left in the cold with a pen

do we remember our bodies when we write?

yesterday, in JT's practice, I could feel all these different points at once, pushing & pulling, in multiple ~~feel~~ relations.

can i summon that as i sit here,
in relationship to material & immaterial objects
places
feelings
?

tara is off against the wall, she makes a soft sound in her throat.

my left foot presses down into the floor. the back of my ~~left~~ right calf presses into my left knee (see, i even get my own limbs mixed up.) i am aware of the distance ~~between~~ ~~m~~ along my neck to my right shoulder as my head tilts to the left. my breath is shallow & my spin dull achy in the middle of my back.

where are we today? as part as crowd

Thursday 6^15 dt

Fear ~~in~~ anticipation of BEAR

Listening

distraction by the nats

I seem to follow JSC in writings — perhaps im wrong but it feels this way. In a nice way!

A NAP was good. Restructuring a brainstorming ideas was interesting. It feels a little strange to end with a performance but then again what isn't performance. I echo Jaime's need for solitude in the midst of everything. There is a beautiful intensity & joy with this group that makes me want these cross pollinations to happen more. It feels brief. like an extended amuse bouche a tasting.

SEEING

another practice to return to.
letting the eyes rest on something for an extended time

TEMPORAL SHIFTS

david sits at the head of the long table
turned towards the wall
1/2 banana & PB sandwich & a few sighs

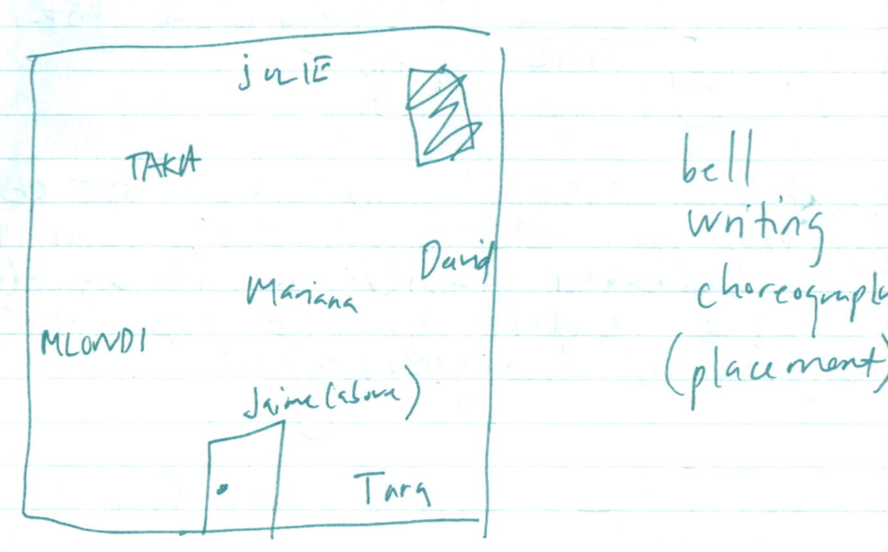

Changes:

— mlondi turns to his side, one leg bends at hip to frame floor
— marias splays her legs, grabs green & white roller to hold up her upper body
— david is up, 2 seconds before the bell

i can't see tara but earlier i saw her by the door curled over her knees

I took photos —

why am i pulled to document this?

jsc 6/14
10:00 am

It all goes so quickly & we are suddenly negotiating the creation of an event/occasion

I miss the discovery of the first day. THE SPACE.

THERE YOU ARE
DIANE MAC'NTYRE W/ ABBY & MAX
DENSE FRUIT UNDER WIRE

STRAWBERRY LETTER 22

KNEES KNOCKED
SITTING ON PORCH THE BELL SINGING
AND SINGING
THOMPSON SAYS THAT. VIBRATION MAKES TONE.
ROOM CHANGES.

"ROOM FOR EVERYONE, ROOM FOR EVERYONE"
PRINCESS XOKIA

T.A. WILLIS PERPENDICULAR, A BLOOM.
ZINNIA-LIKE
FOLDS AND FOLDS OF CURVED UNDERSTANDING
HERE TO FIND A PRIZE —
BUT THE ONE SUMBERGED IN THE WORD
IMPROVIZED

YESTERDAY I SOUGHT OUT THE THING TITLED
"RED" ___. EYES TRAINED ON
STALKS STURDINESS RIPENESS READY FOR
TOUCH N PULL OR PLUCK OR CUT
ALWAYS THE CUT. SEEKS THE RED
AND THE FAMILIAR TURNED TO FABULCATION.
CHARD SOFTENED TO SORREL.
TIME LEMONED TO TAKA'S SALTY SCENTING
WHAAT? I KNOW WHO READS THE PINK RIGHT NOW
I LOVE THE YOUTHFUL BELLY ON THE COUCH I KNOW WHO'S
— WHO'S GOT MY BACK — WE KEEP THE
MOTTLED LIGHT ON AND SKIN CRINKLES

WITH THIS RADICAL SPACE OF MERELY
STARTING (TOGETHER)

HERBALS AWAIT. GROWTH TASTES PEPPERY &
THE SMOKEY PALE GREEN TRAILS, LINGERS.
THESE COULD BE "SKILLS THAT COULD
BE PRACTICED" (← page 1)
THESE ARE THE THINGS OF THE WAKE

DIANE'S MOVEMENT CAUGHT BETWEEN SOUNDS
MOVEMENT SOUNDS LIKE *that* (italics)

IT'S CONTAINED, NOT CAPTURED
I'M SO DOWN WITH THAT
YOU HAVE TO WANT TO KNOW
& KNOW TO ASK
AND ASK TO OPEN
& COLLAPSE TO GROUND
FOR GROUND TO OPEN
FOR THE STRAIN TO LEAN &
HOLD TIGHT A JUICY LIQUID
TRANSFORMING INTO SWEETNESS

MACINTYRE'S BODY A SATURATED SOUNDING
IT RELEASED SOMETHING INTO THE
SOUND AS WELL
THEY SHE
A STAIN
A TERRAIN DETERRORITIALIZED DETONATED
THE PATRIARCHIAL BOMB

THE BARBED COVER.

FOOTSTEPS TRAIL SO WE CAN HEAR THE
BELL. A SOMETHING IS COMING
& IS MOVING AMONGST US, GARDEN. FEELING FOR
THE SUN.

[JT WED 10A]

A dance of listening. Listening, in and of itself as a dance

What does it mean to foreground a listening practice in dance process / composition / workshopping / making? I mean REALLY foreground a listening practice, rigorously, attentively?

Listening itself would be the dance occasion, about decibels vibrating from gut to gut. It probably would be frustrating, as on the surface it would seem like nothing is happening.

(John Cage approached this question in 4'33")

If people came to see a dance and all that was, there was a listening dance, what would be the reaction.

The case we are making here is not about re-creating sound art (although there are clear parallels) More like LISTENING ART, ~~rather~~ rather than sound art.

↳ so what would shift perhaps is the perceived passiveness of listening. (of course listening is always already active, even in our sleep.

Mondi, 2pm
14 June

LIVING ROOM
1

"It's not as though I felt my body. It's not like I will ever return. In a room, where midnight blue coats the wall, and a black light is bolted to the ceiling, a shirt glows white. A horizon of two bulbs cut the room to a yellow painted galaxy in the corner. Not from day light or window, I escape flourescence."

—Ronaldo V. Wilson
<u>Poems of the Black Object</u> p. 13

A black light makes a T-shirt glow.

Polar bears have black skin.
Their fur is clear but presents as white.
Are polar bears Black?

A starry night makes the sky
look ~~distant~~ almost boyant
dynamic
as some stars glow brighter than others making them appear closer or far away. It gives the idea that the night sky is gooey or gel-like as if the stars are not surrounded by the sky but as if the stars are pressed into the black "skin" of the sky.

This pen is some shade of blue.
I prefer a purple ink fountain pen.
This is gel ink.
In the 90s, I used to gel my hair.

When you put gel in black hair, eventually it makes flakes and the gel looks like ash or fake snow in your hair.

This happens when you try to touch or change the fixed and geled hair. like, once you've made up your mind with a gel hair-do, it ruins the appearance of the do when you try to change it. Flakes in black hair are obvious.

Oil is better, but in the 90s I was still learning how to find my best hair style.

There are new paint colors in this house that weren't here the last time I visited.

The stairs are blue and the floor upstairs is black. The blue of the stairs is not the same as the blue of this pen.

In my room, there is a small business card that is a perfect square. There is an image on one side of it and writing on the other. The image side is of my friends at their wedding. They were married here and they are Lesbians.

I hope to see a bear while I'm here. ~~At~~ least a cub. When someone sees a cub, they must be careful because it means that the mom is near by. So when I see the cub (I hope so) I might also see the mom. I'm wishing for a lot out of this potential sighting.

My bruises are healing they hurt less but look worse.
they are blue and purple and look like hell. by: MV 6-12-19

Wait.
They do not want to be as free as you'd make them. Free not as a destiny, but perhaps a different starting point. A starting point which in and of itself would be the end, rather than a starting point after the end. I hear Aime Césaire, always, saying:

"The only thing worth beginning is the end of the world"

These words always invite a collective cultural repression, a refusal to heed the call. What we see instead is a papering over, a kind of make-up application, a cultural cosmetic bandage, an aestheticization of the call, as if it was meant only for aesthetics.

They / We do not want to be as free as that call would make us. So we repress, make whole what is

Towards the end of the day, my words start to dry out.
Writing towards a collective project
means writing towards + among + according to a bell
We are growing seven sibling notebooks
This day has been exhausting in the best way
Pushing + pulling against each other, revealing tender spots
+ strong commitments. I must confess something to you:
THIS IS NOT A MUJI PEN. I'm sorry, I left mine in
the studio. It's hard to keep track of everything. One of
the forms of wiseness I hold most highly is the awareness
of how much one can hold. I often try to do too much
at once + end up rushing.
We were asked by Julie to apply pressure for 20 minutes.
Three people meshed together - in ways that usually only
lovers, siblings, close friends might be. Something so familiar
about that slight shift that happens within intimacy
between affection + struggle. tenderness + suffocation.
[JSC 6/12 6:15pm]

Things we need to, I need to, keep in mind as I carve out my path of contemporary performance and contemporary art as a sustaining artist in the states.

- Don't take yourself and your practice lightly.
- Don't take yourself and your practice too seriously to the point that it suffocates you.
- Keep track of your interest.
- Don't let other people's value dictate and evaluate your worth
- Connect with people as much as possible
- Learn to hold the boundary to protect yourself
- Ask questions. If you can't to that particular person, ask around for advice.
- Incubate your ideas until you're ready to share it.
- Protect and treasure your people.
- Learn to let go
- ....
- ....
- ....

These are a few that just came up in a conversation that happened in a living room, just now.

Lots of frustration. Performance / movement artists are so vulnerable to others around us. That's partly because our work is not valued and evaluated well in the society. Not so tangible. Very ephemeral. Defy capitalization. Time-crossing. The societal value is not suitable so much.

That's another reason why I stick with this medium.

This concept of "entertainment" is something at the core of it all. It is an ideology. The value system for "entertainment".

"Value": I think about how this word has anything to do with art. I don't know

Taka. 6/13/19 2pm

…nging body and mind (do we really need to do that THING? haven't we done plenty of white feminist dance theorizing about their now distinction already?) into focus today, or move accurately all of my parts + onion skin layers, some crisp, some sweet, some on the verge of tears. Last night messed and blend + … + have zero M's in my name) covered all of colonialism with maps and diagrams + post-it note charts around the table. Our reading + history lesson memories categories. My unconsciousness sticks out like a sore thumb, though Mariana says hers does too. More like mine feels unavoidable, mine has taken time to study closely + precisely the black/white parameters U.S.'s of Americans even know exists (+ they don't seem to know much). When we're trying to trace a different + more holistic geography for how people uprooted somebody's homeland + other people violently across miles + miles, that U.S. binary, known intimately to a degree by all of us, doesn't hold up in court. Doesn't add much to what we already know. I know a small hangover when I see one.

from the studio
TAU 2.14.19
10am

A short nap for a short person.

We sat in the unknown today.

Perhaps for the first time this week.

It was scary for some and for some not so scary.

It's because of the body and its precarity.

Tara and I suggested this activity.

Improvisation is hard to manage when you don't "say" that's what's happening.

Flailing.

I smell like food. I ate too fast.

It tasted— good?

last night I learned that it's either OSU

or The Ohio State University

—MLONDI clarified this for me.

♡MV 6-14-19, 2pm

open caucus
caucus fly revelation
overt revere on hold
rapture
release revelation overture
ample for the picking
as cotton as synthetic
verses versus overture
robust answers hold over and refuse
and and and
word at the hold
anchor these things fly or set sail and
this list only holds exposure
free fall is cliché
the fat fecund hand hold
overhead
and and thank you for your coming
anthill or mole the risk
taken by a neck
cacophony freak and the still water
unnecessary chokehold has held the stage lip
for decades but still she scatters
bread for his doorway shadow to partake
and return this disgust regresses
reguet egress egle regalia find
your way out or home to finesse the
ending of your unanswered friend fallen
over backwards she'll tell you again she will
or else
marinate this forehead
sweat relegates itself to the chin or nothing
dances
move and remove again to a fingernail
nonsense is
the best remedy for anxiety

Pressing
and The feeling of squeezing

the big pile of "The Pressure" made me feel like I couldn't press.

Instead I let them squeeze me and layer on top.

I kept getting expressed outward onto Jaime's limbs and I squeezed the calves The Thighs.

Her father had a stroke last night, she said.

Garbled speaking was the code to identify The stroke.

Foundations for communities share what you know don't perpetuate the blind looking seeking structure Go figure it out yourself kind of Thought — tell Them what you didn't know. Even if at times its the blind leading the blind. Take the time to share and it will teach you something too.

This is my favorite/familiar pressure:

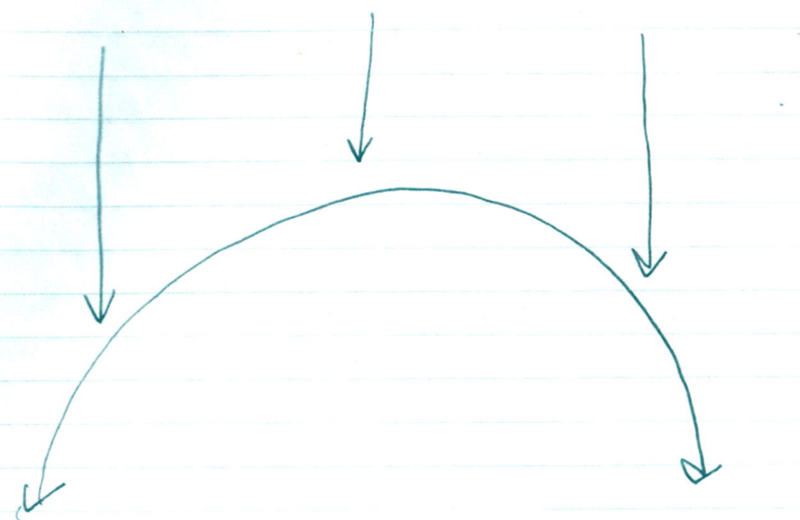

I'm the

in the picture

LIVING ROOM
2

I think i've always felt the abyss as abyssmal, as a falling out of and into - isolation/nothingness lack of control of function or direction i remember using that word with my therapist because it's what came into myself. Keeling writes that the abyss is ~~also~~ "a projection and a perspective into the unknown" (54). "we know ourselves as part + as crowd" (54) she says - singularity & collectivity: both of which have the capacity to support or strangle or desert. having "a" perspective into the unknown" ~~reminds me that~~ makes me think of the spatialization of time as well as the way relationship (time, space, social position) creates our understandings of our own position. (Stuart Hall) Keeling uses the metaphor of a boat, also a spaceship. crowded vessels where we each look forward into the unknown we find - what will we find? [jsc]

Maybe today there's a way of removing the obstinate feeling of being overcome by an absent thing, intangible and lingering. Useful, the mountain floating like a line crafted by a giant over horizon, for keeping things at bay. What's left? Nothing but the way a body falls into a chair with such conviction in its own familiar shape. Recreating the sitting that made the hips ache in the first place - "familiar" is the easiest way. I keep thinking I should quote somebody. Or write a line that uses all the research I've done. But I keep disassociating into rambles and weird-ish grammar, as if trying to ease a boulder out of the forest floor or a lid off a heavy pot to let out worms or steam - as if ignoring what I'm saying might get me to what I'm not able to say.

"this is why we stay with poetry.

thinking now about
TAW 6.12.19
2pm

And just like that it decomposed. Not because it had form before. No. It didn't. That's what was great. The intensification of that lack of form. But decomposition is too filled with cycles of life. Maybe putrefaction is the word. Maybe rot. Maybe just like that it began to rot. To rot without potential for recomposition.

This particular stitch is the lie @ the center of everything. It is Narcissus masturbating with a mirror. It is Narcissus as the lunar eclipse, occluding, displacing, obscuring, obstructing, concealing. The chorus sings a sheeply tune. The ampitheater is filled with fog machines. The audience chokes while masturbating while covering eyes. The theater is the birth of the clinic. The theater is the lie at the center of putrefaction.

The chorus is still choking.

MB.2. 6pm

Today its rainy the opposite of yesterday's weather. We don't know really what Jaime + Tara will teach us or lead us through today. Yesterday we went through the seven past generations with Taka, Negative spase with Mondli, translation of text with David, lifting each other up with me, and applying pressure with Julie.

My body needed rest after all of that. It was spiritually, academically, creatively and socially stimulated. I loved it. It felt like a "Natural Generation."

This is something I wrote down when we did Mondli's class. Julie is writing upside down on the opposite page right now. She couldn't find a book in time. It feels like sharing a slate in an old school house.

I just stared out the window for a long time and the green leaves burned into my eyes. I'm choosy (sp?) when it comes to liking or disliking rainy days— it all depends on my emotional weather. Today, I like the rain. ♡ MV 6-13-19, 10am

→ thank you Manara for the desk ♡

I peeked and in the
#1 living room

there was a special naming

fist bump to MV as we write side to side – struck in house @ record kell / we

I M P R O V I S E

This was listed a 7 SIBLINGS.

7 sibling notebooks finding the way to each other & thru each other

(~~[illegible]~~ consider how this relationality ~~[illegible]~~ could be

de - familiar - ized

to keep open spaces for other KIN FOLK & kin / relation - ability.

Like the 'negative nancy' (MLONDI term) I am the 'debbie downer' – or better said by ~~[illegible]~~ —

~~THE~~ KILL JOYS ~~A~~ are in the house – or perhaps that is / our term

KILL JOY ERIZED

Upside down & backwards & late and in the future
spit/live space dead space body space

JT [illegible] 10 AM

JSC Thurs 2pm

Anger and frustration was coming out of the room. To honor our practice and artistry. To sustain our integrity

DET

And im still angry. I connect the plight of artists at ~~times~~ times to the civil rights era. Where it is assumed that certain people are not valuable and don't deserve compensation.

Privilege
the right to demand for yourself and not be concerned with others.

desserts with others
—read over Mariana's shoulder

We are constantly asked for so much — to justify our existence and projects and needs. To be told ~~that~~ 'we can't cover that', 'it's not in our budget.' Okay this is not the place for me to vent.

Joy — where to find joy and how to make it more present in life?

SLEEP
REST
VACATION
REJUVENATION

how do we, as artists look at these things

Being present w/ CATALYZING STRUCTURES here!

The country air makes me want to lie down.
Are we workaholics unconsciously?
Even with long breaks (2hrs?) in the middle of the day i have to refuel — working until 10pm or rather

reorganize the next day. What seems fair in this process?
I don't have a true barometer
I'm just in my own space
with my own needs.

addendum — there is no judgement — just thoughts. -

Collective thinking. Radical Listening. Mlondi brought up this idea: Radical listening. This group of people, each extremely thoughtful, invested maker themselves, is the beautiful example of Radical listening. The active, responsive, accountable listening that happens in the room is so inspiring. It makes me want to be generous.

Listening and investment. Being invested in what you listen or who to listen to. The response to the listening, both in a discussion and as a response to the proposition, is radical, radical listening. I never thought of willingness to an action as so connected to the listening.

It takes energy. Being attentive takes energy. Being invested in an action takes energy.

At a first class of acting course, it always ~~???~~ starts with "learning how to listen." There is a reason for that.

Taka 6:10 pm. 6/13/19

P.S. Selective listening, yes we are always editting out what we want to hear. Being selective. Sometimes, we hear ~~what~~ only what we want to hear. Sometimes, we believe only what we want to believe. ~~The~~ Listening and desire. Desire to hear. Hearing only what we are ~~out~~ comfortable with. Being brave enough, being open enough, to listen and invest in what makes me uncomfortable. That's hard, but we ought to do it. If I am interested in the "conversation" and "relations" with others, I need to open up my channel without ~~being~~ losing my core, my self. That's important. Important for me to be involved in a society, to be in a relationship with others.

I have a desire to be upside down. The fever I have is excruciating, making me want to be upside down, head resting on the ground. If I am to function at all, I have to be upside down.

→ The body has its will. Sometimes the body wills against your desire, wills against your own desire. It shuts down and says no even when you wanna keep going.

Contamination — Bacteria, infection, transmission, incubus, virus, antibodies, medicine, herbal tea, ginger, honey, Benadryl, 2 tablets 3 times a day, drowsiness, fever, runny nose, don't touch others, quarantine, don't contaminate others, don't spread the sickness.

Care for thyself, don't be a burden, don't be a "prima donna", don't let others see you weak, keep pushing (slow down!), take the medicine that will slow you down,

that makes you feel like shit. It really feels like death. This has to stop This has to stop this has to stop this has to stop this has to stop this has to stop this has to stop this has to stop this has to stop this has to stop this has to stop this
has to

to stop

stop this

has

to

STOP

(Monday, 14 June
10am)

IN LIGHT OF THE OCCASION

OF MAR DEL PLATA

JT 2PM 14 JUNE

pg 124 Chapter THE OTHER DOOR

My current ~~title~~ title of a new work

who is called on to disappear?

Social fabric is thus held in suspension

fear agony guilt anxiety trouble pervasive malaise

The living become untimely disappeared potential speakers

it is a question of slow poisoning a delayed psychic bomb

Identity is changed it becomes hyphenated

(in the sentence "she's no longer suffering" to what, to whom does "she" refer?

What does that present tense mean?,

12. BARTHES cover txt

I'M LISTENING TO THINKING & WRITING & BODIES & PAPER ACTIVE MOTION & MARIANA'S POSITIVE SIGH THE ROOM SPEAKS AS A DOOR THE BELL TRILLS. VALVE IS CHANGED INTO ALL THOSE BOOKS THOUGHTS THE ROOM AWAKENS BOOKS CLOSE ON THE SOUND OF WRITING WANDERING NECESSITY

(1997/11) p.124 AVERY GORDON'S GHOSTLY MATTERS

June 1 Sat 10a (dt)

The Scent of Palo Santo.
the clearing
the burning
the chemical & mental shifts
the reminder

frustrating conversation w/ website hosting & pricing. Basically how they control the information to guide you to their needs. No transparency in pricing / options / information. You must rely on a person who themselves is working with algorhythms to create more profit.
Earlier Kitchen conversation with Julie & Mariana about economics of artmaking and negotiation. Who is the ecosystem serving and where is the transparency?

CONFLICT RESOLUTION ⟶ LISTENING

I hear MLONDI's voice in prior writings and empathize with her sickness & frustration. I don't feel it directly but on one level i do feel the moment. This doesn't make sense. But i understand. Opacity & transparency within.

Yolanda walked in to make breakfast.
The entry of another being that shifts the

air. Adds another narrative.

Starch in your shirt

used for crispness & definition
a stiffening
form builder
additive
heat sensitive
TYPE OF FOOD that fills one up
DIETARY AVOIDANCE
insult
comment
metaphor

We are negotiating words that don't have natural transparencies. They live as signs & symbols, ideas, images, misunderstandings and sonic utterances. They live in and outside of context. Framed and on a broad field

Ingredients of perception

STATES OF MIND AND BODY

THIS IS A FRAME

O THIS IS A FRAME

THIS IS A FRAME

this is
a frame

THIS IS
A FRME

STUDIO LOFT

til now what I would do for a person — not a field, or an idea, or a movement, or a million losing souls, or a form, or the memory of someone blown up large. But a person right before me. This is how we all get better, I suppose. By caring so hard we push at our own edges.

TAW

TENDER ♡

It's when someone asks you to pause — you feel both foolish & grateful. foolish because you hadn't realized how rush & forward-motion you were being, and in the process not actually aware of this moment this body & god forbid, even these feelings. grateful of course, because you were reminded, you got another chance, to start again. "begin again, again" — one of my favorite doug powell aphorisms. i hear a plane passing — i wonder if anyone else is registering that. reminds me of the scene(s) in mrs. dalloway, when the plane passes above, and we see into the minds of so many people who stop to notice the same thing. oh modernism. There is so much to take in here — this place, all of us, the indefinite shape of something to be made together. at once not enough & too much. I wish there was a way for us to work together that allowed for us to bring along all of our minor & major dramas — to not feel like they had to be put on a shelf. i can feel their presence as shadows, hovering. my stomach is full, i am standing at a lectern, which is perhaps my new favorite writing position. "how is your heart?" someone asked me that once, casually, like instead of how are you, and it made me feel both tender & afraid.

wednesday 6 15 (dt)

the brain and body trust — TRUST. A strange combination of letters. Foundation, holding space, belief.

THE TIES THAT BIND TO CREATE MEANING. THAT ENTANGLE OUR SENSES IN WAYS THAT SEEM BEYOND US UNTIL WE GO RENEGADE ~~AND~~ OR AWOL.

MY HAND IS CRAMPING AGAIN AND I TRY TO FIND EASE IN THIS PROCESS.

DRAWING SYMBOLS

&

SIGNS

WHAT IS THE SEMIOTICS OF WRITING? THE IDENTITY OF OUR SCRIPT, THE FORM OF OUR LETTERS. BREAKING PASS THE BORDERS OF EACH LINE. I NOTICED MY MOTHER'S HANDWRITING WHEN I WAS A CHILD. SHE GREW UP IN JAMAICA. There was a distinctive form to her letters & cursive — which they no longer teach to kids in school now. I came to call her script colonial because i noticed that only those from former colonised countries ~~had~~ used this script. Other islands in the Caribbean, those from India, Pakistan and other parts of Africa.

An almost invisible sign / remnant —

I moved the loft space to the living room
a portable living room # 3
to accomodate food and the return of the dishes
The mundane changes us so "radically"
the good of kind of
breaking rules
taking value(?) risks
of where to be and live
with what cream rises — The way I feel about
oh yes → reminds me of India Arie
"Brown Skin" —
back to morning practice
of feeling cold
being up all hours & wee hours ~~too~~ then
body —
I cant say body without it ~~potten~~ potent
potential to empty

Dancer's are so body vital. I hope you see how
that works outside of the bubble outside
of health. I say you — I mean that for
me too.
Virtuosity through survival.
Maybe its a 50s thing though I ~~call~~ call it
a cool 100 yrs old.
Body reorganized by pressure (that's downward &
upward)

Hot salsa spicy chips on northern beans & greens.
eaten w/ a spoon.

Cross Cultural Culinary ... all leftovers
the LEFTOVERS →
"El Sobrante"

JT. 2:16 pm. 13 JUNE

♡ MV 6-13-19
6 pm

I came to see some green, I saw some green and sheen. My brain is tired and like a teen.

Teenagers go for it. They don't have frontal cortex yet formed. The floor in this studio is heated. I think they call it radiant floor.

I wanna fuck shit up.

I have gas from the beans. Bought limes at Sunflower Market. Three cheers for the honey comb bunch!

Saw two hogs today. HedgeHogs in the hedge.

what if I wrote this small does it sound tiny in your brain?
Do I sound like a tape recorder in fast forward?
Do I sound like a mini answering machine tape in fast forward?

HOW ABOUT NOW? HOWABOUTNOW?!

Measuring. Measuring. I keep bringing back this idea of measuring of time. When the time is measured, it compartmentalizes this abstract existence that's always there: second, minute, hour, day, week, month, year...

This division of time is useful, for our sanity (thinking about solitary confined prison cell), for the society (uniform understanding and scheduling with others), and for the effecacy of energy consumption (how long to do what activity)...

At the same time, it functions well with productivity-focused capitalism, which makes me feel skeptical for a sec. I keep telling myself being productive is not an evil, something to avoid (have to avoid); however, it does make me stop. Who am I kidding,... After a second of questioning, I move on and still trive for the most efficient and productive approach to thing. That's just how I am wind-up to be.

Back to the topic. The difference between Kronos time and Kairos time: the alpha-wave inducing physical state: restoration, where time (division of time) doesn't chase me after,.. I dont need to .... well the bell is ringing. External reminder of time just like sun sets down and the sun comes out. Season.

Taka 10 am 6/14/19

jsc 6/14 2:00pm

just landed out of lunch
being together in the studio like this
makes it a library
SHHHHHHH
so quiet, but we aren't allowed to sleep yet.

mañana
can
fall
asleep
any
time

taka
thinks
about
time
a
lot

i
like
to
make
jokes
about
thyme

we're
out
of
thyme
again

julie just inquired about time
as it is measured in days
fourteen
i'm glad i'm not that age
even though it's much farther from
the end of life
barring exceptions of course

i heard the idea that holding on to old experiences
~~[illegible]~~ prevents the present newness (used time)
to register + leave an imprint.
i feel that to be true. i'm often comparing
new experiences + old ones in ways that
restrict + circumscribe. i lose out. i take
away the possibility of surprise.

AW
6.15.19
10 am

foreclosing the possible outcomes
predetermine and then follow through up to a point
predetermine at least a direction and the allow
in "nevermind"
from here I can see an oval, seats surrounding + surrounded
by possible outcomes, changed + changing forward
the way things linger in the next and the next thing.
what changes when you see from above, from the rafters?
things sound different
look like a whole
look like the bottom half of the frame with these
wooden tents and lines and vacant spaces and fans
ready to spin.
this is a frame in the way a proscenium tries to be
the eye is a frame in the way a proscenium
longs to be: flexible and mobile, the illusion of
movement and consistent equilibrium even as
things change by magic or otherwise

today reality seeps in a bit.
or maybe unreality.
who comes. the boundaries aren't real,
only in language + that satisfying feeling
of having articulated something clearly.
addictive + productive ... also
requires attention
to non-clarity
continue to be paid

I have an application due, for which I finally
looked through the work sample video - the
beginnings of the research were more
robust + deeply embodied + choreographically
clear than I remembered. I guess that
can happen when a dance is built from

multiple years of doing a specific set of scores but also built in four days with sound designer just before opening night. There were things I ~~couldn't~~ hadn't remembered & things that seem much more important now than they might have as I was doing them.

What I'm afraid of is my project description. What is it, though? That's hard to write when I have only been writing about other people's work so much. What is mine? What do I want for it? What can it become & where has it landed now?

Mariana said there is a frenetic thing at my core as a performer that doesn't always come out w/out seeing me in specific work. I think this is true.

TIME:

15 MIN

SPACE

7 PAST 12

AFTERNOON

SATURDAY

in "ren test"

PORCH

The scene is like the Sentence: structurally there is no obligation for it to stop; no internal constraint exhausts it. . . No scene has no meaning, no scene moves toward an enlightenment or a transformation. The scene is neither practical nor dialectical; it is a luxury and idle: as inconsequential as a perverse orgasm: it does not leave a mark, it does not sully . . . the scene recalls the Roman style of vomiting: I tickle my uvula (I rouse myself to contestation), I vomit (a flood of wounding arguments), and then, quite calmly, I begin eating again

– Roland Barthes, A Lover's Discourse, p.206-7

WEDNESDAY 10[05] (dt)

FIVE CONSTELLATIONS
FIVE PILLS
FIVE SPIRIT GUIDES
FIVE SENSES
FIVE LOVERS

The roar of a distance waterway echoes in the hills.
Pink peonies are my companions, Tumeric my helper.
Oatmeal with nuts ~~and~~ dried fruit, honey and cream, my ground.

Tumbling down a mountain. Falling like a child
on the soft earth in the sunshine. I have forgotten
joy. The line between fear and joy can be thin.
Two sides of the same coin — it all depends on
how you flip the moment. A metaphor of freedom
or despair.

I see the sun.
assembling my senses to focus on the warmth
that envelopes me
The soft wind
The clarity of light
The ~~scent~~ fecund scent of earth
Sucking on a stone
waiting

return
reiterate
refuse
refine
redact
regulate
reserve
wrong
wrote
~~right~~
resist
replay
render
Rolf
rouse
arouse
everything pushing upon me, it happens with the open space so many directions the leaves capturing exactly that a roar that becomes less and less and less like the water that is – supposedly is.
to ~~uncen~~ uncenter me is to lose me, to be unseen and perhaps to disentangle from the world apart or maybe to be of the world and not the one that organizes it
there is a nature not "natural" – in spell thinking about the ~~[illegible]~~ non neutral nature, the land racialized by labor, primarily the context of the color line, the predetermination

what do I know of the sun? it will go that way – it will hover higher or lower from season to person (season looks like person)

how much I enjoyed watching you, and you x6. to be of your voice – the ones on the inside
for this I return, reiterate, refuse, refine, redact, arouse and tickle within me the wound. this wound. a sound.

JT
porch bench
2pm

And more pressure.

we lifted up we saw negative space
we saw the unseen by pressing into what
is already there.
this is a fountain pen. I lost the Muji pen.
That pen was gel.

The bear walks around like its used to
People. it is used to people coming in
and out of the studio.
The bear was a medium size. Dark brown
fur. I was writing about polar bears earlier
and I wonder what color the skin of
a brown bear might be.
A polar bear has black skin.

it smells like potato startch on this porch.
I wonder if we will eat potatos for
dinner.

It's interesting to hear gun shots in

this countryside.

My sister hears them all the time in chicago. She says that each week, there is a tally of all the people who have gotten shot that week or weekend I cannot remember which. in any case last week or weekend, 28 people were shot in Chicago.

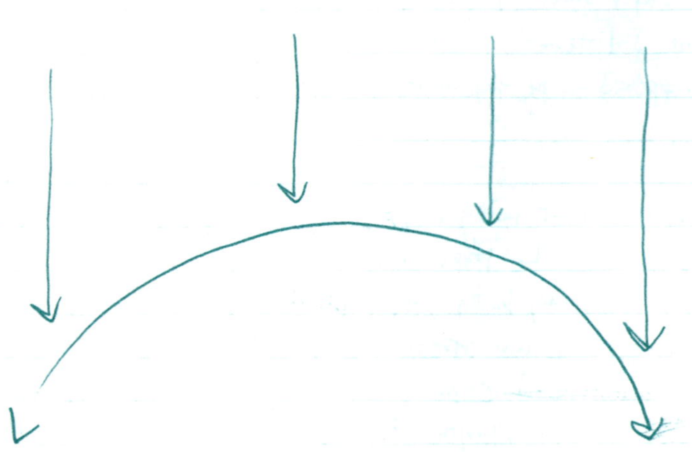

That is my favorite position in Julie's pressure work we did today. i am the in the drawing.

it felt familiar it doesn't mean I liked it it just felt like life. Perhaps just my life. Lift up lift your self up

lift up the ones who need lifting.

lift up through gravity

gravity is in each of us.

DO YOUR PART ♡ MV 6-12-19, 6pm.

The Lord is...

the law
the testimony
the unseen
the ghost
the guilty
the evidence
the judge
the testimony
the police
the cathedral
the panopticon
the prison
my shepherd
the will
the way
the make-belief
the mystery
the myth
the court
the bias
the daddy
the Norm
the behavior modification
the Power
the Glory
Bio power
morning glory
The creator
the creation story
The Alpha (male)
The end
The savior
The Touch
The Scream
The truth
The Head of State
The Prohibition
The sculptor

the fetishist
The Master
Dominatrix
The Penis
The seminal
The Only
The Beard
The Robe
The Homosexual
The Voice
The Reason
The North
The Universe
The Brains
The Highest
The Redeemer
The forgiver
The Punisher
The scolder
The comforter
The Balm
The Top

Mandi
2pm / 13 June

Will we make anything?
I wrote her a poem and sent it in a text. She said it was the best poem anyone has written her.
She left and packed and didn't get to do her laundry. She likes to do her laundry before she leaves town because it helps her have less laundry when she returns. it's part of her preparation of departure.

The mushroom soup was delicious last night. She is doing mushrooms while at the beach This weekend. I have never done mushrooms but I am willing to try them — I suppose I should say or could say — I am curious to try them. I'm a little afraid of what they will reveal. Kind of like when I smell or inhale sage. It makes me feel sick and like I am going to throw up. Its a nauseating feeling/Encounter. Someone used to say to me that it was because I have a lot of demons. I don't believe that demons could do that. If I have a lot of Them, then I should be used to feeling them. I know the demons.

Suddenly, I'm missing ALL of my dead people.

♡ mv 6-14-19
10 am

on their behalf & w/out permission, assuming motherhood & womanhood as designated pregnancy, or at the very least manufacturing pity for parents who either are involved "in any one person's choice ("mother's" everywhere suddenly standing in for each individual pregnant person. Conjuring sameness out of the singularity of experience in a word. Conjuring a "should" where there might instead be an "if" or something else altogether(?).

the steps of the studio are almost like the porch.
i wanted to be outside.
sometimes i don't listen fully & then i end up in situations i have agreed to but don't want
sometimes i become the brat character in a group
it is not really a role i like or resonate with much anymore. i was much more of a brat a decade ago. sometimes when i actually need or want things. i express them in sarcastic ways, or jokey ways. why am i processing in this notebook. i would rather write something thoughtful / lyrical / profound / charming.

just listen to the wind

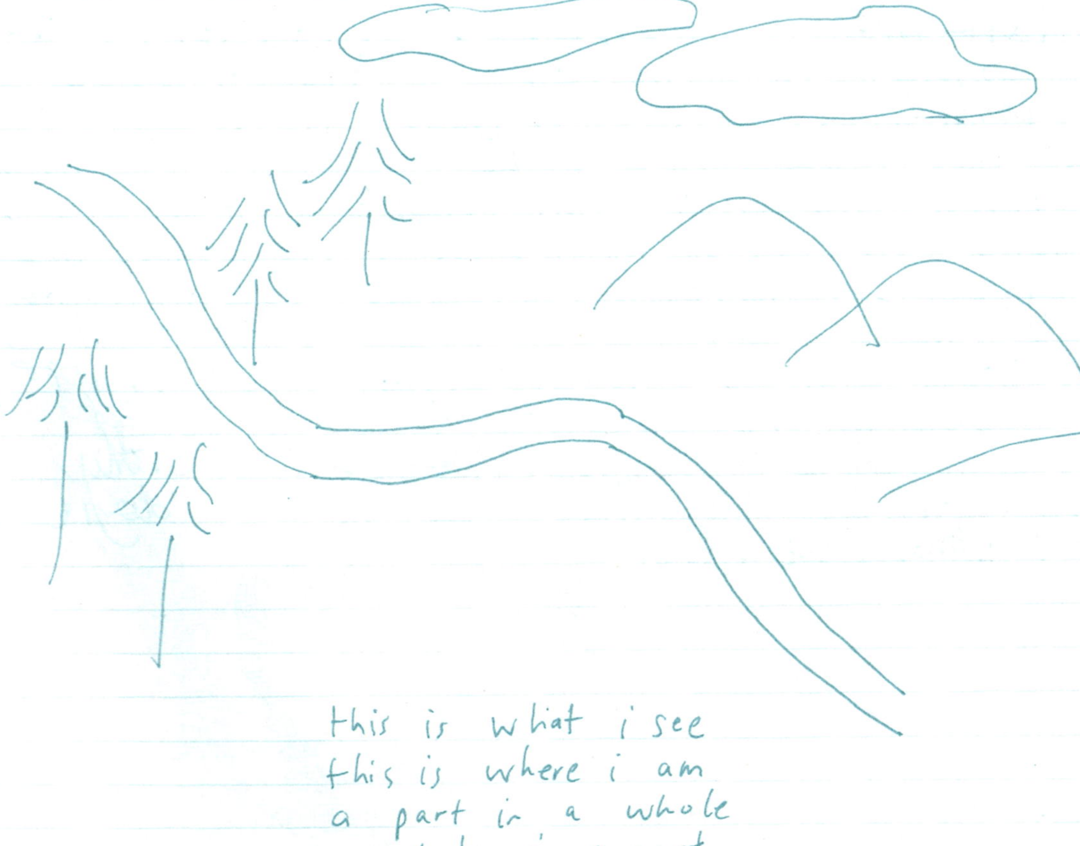

this is what i see
this is where i am
a part in a whole
a whole in a part

JSC
6/19/19
6:00 pm

STUDIO

22 I KNOW ABOUT THE WILL, ITS SELFISHNESS, IT'S ENTIRE
GREED: HOW IT IS A DARK POWER, A MOON,
AND IS SUPREME, SIR, A BLUE AND UTTERMOST FICTION

I will not pledge allegiance to country, soldiers, parades; — their doctors, nurses, priests, police, mayors, managers, (same thing). Disneyland, Ivy League, American Idol, church, Pride parades, the newspaper — They all seduce me. The protest. Even the protest. Especially the protest. I will not focus ~~on~~ solely, on the leader. The leader, donning his rich Dutch colors, leaving an acidic citrus burn on every skin — is not the focus, is not the only focus. The leader is all of us as much as he is against all of us. The leader is not a warlord. We wanted a warlord. The leader warlords our desires. The leader warlords on our behalf. The leader's warlording causes panic and confusion. We obfuscate everything as a result. As if this warlording began now, or yesterday, or two years ago. When in fact this warlording is the heritage, this warlording is the DNA. It is the stitch. It is the blood transfusion. It is the only script. It is every smile, every gesture, the way we swish our hips from side to side. It is the very ground we walk on. It is the climate. It is the atmosphere. It is cellular, It is ~~micros~~ microscopic. It is every sonic vibration. It is every earth shake. It is every bead of sweat. It is every texture. It is the temperature. It is everything. It is every ship, every piece of cotton, every ...

Wednesday 2pm (dt)

I am reminded of a child.
The beauty of not knowing.
The chance to still lay in innocence & wonder in the world
The possibility of transforming an object you don't understand
Mimicking a protocol to engender laughter
Allowing your gaze to rest on something for an interminable
amount of time — without fear or worry.
TIME
the moment

I was watching a bumblebee flying near a hole in a
wooden support beam. For some reason it was trying to
get something in that hole — or get into it. I couldn't
understand but the action was intriguing. persistence

MYSTERY & INTIMACY
unheard whispers — instructions — confidence —
sharing desires. Watching the trust and unexpected
results. Why must we know everything?
How can we sit with just the magic of being?

My hand is cramping.
I reread what was written before —

War violence anger identity tribe politics
personal framing. What if we were to fall asleep
each time we became angry? What would the
world feel like? Where would people sleep?
How would the feel when they woke up?
How would they adjust? Would we still be
slaves or masters? — I mean managers.

I tired — not angry — just weary from many

6:17 pm. 6/12/19

Grappling. Grappling to ...

The heat that I felt from the body of others.
The pressure. that is applied. to my thigh. to my leg. to my arm. to my hand. to my shoulders. to my torso. to my fingers. to my neck. to my chest. to my side of organs.

I am feeling nothing. Nothing of emotion that I can identify.

I am feeling everything. Everything or myriad of pressures that my body can only identify.

My mind is ~~no~~ numb. numb with language, but full of language that are meant for physical communication: relationality without language.

Mlondi showed series of photographs and said, "I think you know what I'm getting at.

Marianna suggests association without clearly saying it. She also couldn't find a word that describes her feelings to bring the pressure upward.

Julie says she usually starts to cry when she experiences something for which she cannot find language.

David suggests "love" and we all agreed on the silence. Silence full of potential, doubt, fear, and profundity.

Jaime talks about the eye-contact that changed Jaime's relationship to collective effort.

Tara talks about the stone that is affected and affecting. Meanwhile, describes the experience of being lifted and association with drawings that are angular on one side but curvy and almost figurative in ~~the abstracted~~ the most abstracted way on the other corner.

I ... words words words. I don't know what to do with my hand, but I don't need to know what to do with it, either.

Taka

→

TAW 6.13.19
10 am

the rush of the Esopus is heavier today with rain but possibly I'm imagining the sound of the expressway — as we say in the midwest — as the sound of rushing water. It feels like a storm coming slowly over a mountain, but the storm is already over us. A trick of echo + reverb + vibration. Space and distance are always different here. I feel it immediately upon arrival, but the fullest attunement to it takes longer to set in.

I am still astonished by the shape the mountain makes by disappearing into the fog + clouds. The sharp rectangles of green through the studio windows, which somehow feels like a density of woods even if I can only see one layer of foliage. Today I'm slow to rise to the occassion. There are a lot of layers to get through toward action. Organizing a sequence of events helps my surface, but maybe it also over-structures. I feel like I'm relearning balance for the first time, but alongside all the knowledge of the past 12 years accumulated, the past six years dragging at my heels, the shift having gotten so slow its been imperceptable until recently. Okay, if everything outside me suddenly changes + the ripple effects of that have mostly taken their course, what am I doing now?

When it rains here, it feels like the world closes in and becomes more outside while I am inside. How spread wide out, with unknown things going on, unsensible causes + effects unfolding, small + large, close by invisible + at a distance, while we huddle, crouching + swimming between these four walls indoors.

Who will come find these notebooks?

In the end of the world or 40 years, who will read + study these ramblings and write the tome on dance + performance in 2019 that digs through all our trash and shit for jewels?

I feel like a difficult person
I am really not a difficult person
I feel like I just presented myself as a diva
I am really not a diva
I feel bad
The bad feeling is paralyzing
I think I need to ~~be~~ quiet
Voice severing
A difficult person's voice must be servered now!
Sever the difficulty
Mute the sound ~~bite~~ byte
Mute the complaining
Suppress the confusion
Swallow the complicated tangled line of questioning
Make America obedient again
Affect travels through voice
Affect is obscured through voice
The esophagus must be pulverized now
Voices of the difficult
Servered at the market square
Voices stuffed like foi gras
paraded at the town square
Difficult esophagus
Call in now.

JT 10AM 14 JUNE

DIFFICULTY BEING
TO BE DIFFICULT
BETTING ON IT
A WOLF'S TEETH
TO BE THE THING
WITHIN THE LAMB
THAT MAKES IT
KICK WITHIN WITHIN
THE WOLF'S TEETH

It's hard not to fall into the liberal space of dance's bounty and privileged sorrow that if we are in it isn't it ours to ponder to make spaces for those who wouldn't survive this covenant yet because you have to learn it unless you are so gifted as to be so smart so sharp so wonderful so kind so nice oh so nice oh so sharp so fierce so [illegible] what is open at this point is it open to miss others' way [illegible] can you are outside of the gaze to be open in the rooms to promise to keep it comfortable or to keep it representing something that's healthy and to protect project what gets learned is that we know a lot about ourselves and I'm so desperate to get close to that which makes people generous and for those of us who can be good at giving it for those of us who are good at giving it for those of us who cannot shape ourselves to fit for those of us who understand spaces that can be connected for those who cannot hear me for me who cannot open up a form that feels open to others I feel bad we all feel so sad all the time all the time all the time mashed and fatty in so many ways this is like how I am full to the brim full fucking filled up with empty filled up with emptiness and a yearning to dearing during it's so hard to say it like being too and being so nothing enough. If nothing a sort of lands but to be nothing to people to have no import my voice is [illegible] with what I cannot touch inside of myself and it's turning me inside out and nothing can reach that dirty inside that dirty unkempt mess of the emptiness that can be filled with random [illegible] and the kinds of sex that happens when I don't have to speak or that my command comes thru a steely attention to myself someone's body. it's been

BUT FIRST ONE MUST FIND OUT IF YOU BELIEVES IN ☐ ← FILL IN.

— TO WHOM GOES THE WILL? —

pressure that I can't give up because it's a weight for an emptiness that makes [illegible]

that is a combat it's being the thing inside the lamb [illegible]

♡ MV 6-14-19,
6pm

Zinc
Charcoal

Yolanda has similar overalls to Jaime

Taka has similar feet to Mariana

David and Tara are tall

Jaime has similar hair to David and Mlondi

Tara has similar hair to Mariana

This room/studio is similar to a Friends meeting.

Julie wears glasses like Mariana
they are not similarly shaped though.

Jaime heard ghosts in the farm house a couple of years ago when he stayed here for a wedding. They stayed here alone.
The ghosts smoked cigs. My kind of ghosts.

I am enjoying this word MYSTERY in this time here. Something that is not explicit. Something that exists but not expressed ~~exist~~ or communicated clearly. Something that leaves space for the spectators to enter into. Something that relies on the opacity. Something that is abstract. Something that is mystical. Something that is metaphysical. Something that came out of an intention / willful / active execution. Something that contains meaning that hasn't been articulated for easy digestion. Something that is trusted, relies on trust. Something that is bigger than / larger than us. Something that makes us (the spectator) want more (or want to sustain in it), but at the same time, makes us go confused and frustrated with ~~exce~~ excessive dose. Something that requires (for me personally) boundary or container, either in terms of time or space or narrative or sequence or energy or attention so that ~~it wo~~ its energy won't lose / dissipate ~~its p~~ itself (and its potency). It is this *something* that is not nothing ~~or~~ nor anything. It is that *some*, a certain *some* that is a *thing* and an event and an atmospher and a connection and a disembodiment and an association and an emotion and a logic / illogic. and an object and an aura and a tension and a body and a space and a reason and an unreason and a purpose and a sound and a shape and and and and and.

JAIME SHEARN COAN is a writer and ACLS Public Fellow at the ONE Archives Foundation. He received his PhD in English from The Graduate Center, CUNY upon completion of his dissertation, "Corporeal Archives of HIV/AIDS: The Performance of Relation." His writing has appeared in publications including *TDR*, *Critical Correspondence*, *Drain Magazine*, *The Brooklyn Rail*, *Movement Research Performance Journal*, *Gulf Coast*, *On Curating*, *Women & Performance*, and *Bodies of Evidence: Ethics, Aesthetics, and Politics of Movement*. He co-edited Danspace Project's catalogue, *Lost and Found: Dance, New York, HIV/AIDS, Then and Now* and is the author of the chapbook *Turn it Over*.

DOROTHY LIN is a graphic designer who collaborates with artists, cultural organizations, and art book publishers. She specializes in typography to create books and exhibition design.

DAVID THOMSON is a collaborative interdisciplinary artist. He has worked with Trisha Brown, Susan Rethorst, Bebe Miller, Remy Charlip, Grisha Coleman|Hot Mouth, Ralph Lemon, Sekou Sundiata, Tracie Morris, Meg Stuart, Marina Abramović, Yvonne Rainer, Yanira Castro, and Kaneza Schaal, among many others. His work engages questions of identity, value, and presence, structuring environments through a range of temporal forms from short works to durational tasks. He received Bessie Awards for Sustained Achievement (2001) and Outstanding Production (2018) for *he his own mythical beast*. Thomson has been recognized with awards and fellowships from US Artist, LMCC, Yaddo, MacDowell, and the Robert Rauschenberg Foundation.

JULIE TOLENTINO (Filipino-Salvadoran) is a movement-based interdisciplinary artist. Recent 2019 commissioned works include *REPEATER*, *.burymefiercely.*, and *Slipping Into Darkness - Day & Night*. Tolentino is a recipient of the Foundation for Contemporary Arts award and was a 2018–2020 UCR Dean's Distinguished MFA Fellow. Many thanks to Jaime, Tara, Mount Tremper Arts, fierce fellow residency comrades, and Dorothy Lin.

MARIANA VALENCIA is a choreographer and performer. Her work has been presented in venues and museums across the United States, England, Norway, Serbia, and Macedonia. Valencia is a Whitney Biennial artist (2019), a Bessie Award recipient for Out-standing Breakout Choreographer (2018), a Foundation for Contemporary Arts Award to Artists grant recipient (2018), and a Jerome Travel and Study Grant fellow (2014–15). She has worked on various performance projects alongside Lydia Okrent, Jules Gimbrone, Elizabeth Orr, Kate Brandt, AK Burns, Guadalupe Rosales, Em Rooney, robbinschilds, Kim Brandt, Morgan Bassichis, Jazmin Romero, Fia Backström, and MPA.

TARA AISHA WILLIS performed in a collaboration by Will Rawls and Claudia Rankine and in The Skeleton Architecture's Bessie Award-winning performance. She is a PhD candidate in Performance Studies at New York University and Associate Curator in Performance & Public Practice at the Museum of Contemporary Art Chicago. Willis has been an editor for *Women & Performance* and *TDR*, co-edited an issue of *The Black Scholar* with Thomas F. DeFrantz, and held a NYPL Jerome Robbins Dance Division Research Fellowship. She was the founding administrator of Movement Research's Artists of Color Council, and was in the first working group for "Creating New Futures," the COVID-19 responsive guidelines for ethical dance presenting.

TAKAHIRO YAMAMOTO is an artist and choreographer based in Portland, Oregon. His performance and visual art works have been presented at PICA, Portland; DiverseWorks, Houston; Contemporary Arts Center, Cincinnati; The Henry Art Gallery, Seattle; and GoDown Arts Centre, Nairobi, among other venues. He is part of the Portland-based support group Physical Education with Allie Hankins, keyon gaskin, and Lu Yim. Yamamoto holds an MFA in Visual Studies from Pacific Northwest College of Art. He is a Full-Time Visiting Artist in the Department of Performance at the School of Art Institute of Chicago in 2020.

MLONDI ZONDI is a US-based South African interdisciplinary artist, dramaturg, curator, scholar, and Robert Rauschenberg Foundation Artist-in-Residence (2020). Mlondi makes performances for the black box theater, gallery/museum, proscenium stage, and other public spaces. This work, often created in collaboration with others, has been presented at the Durban Art Gallery, The Market Theatre (Johannesburg), ICA Live Art (Cape Town), Laguna Art Museum, Axis Lab Chicago, Museum of Contemporary Art Chicago, San Francisco Museum of Modern Art, Mount Tremper Arts, Gibney New York, and the African Burial Ground in New York City.

Marking the Occasion

Document Series #5
First Edition, 2020
Edition of 300 copies
ISBN: 978-1-7327086-9-3
Library of Congress Control Number: 2020943139

Edited by Jaime Shearn Coan and Tara Aisha Willis
Editorial assistance by Rachel Valinsky
Copy editing by Corinne Butta and Rachel Valinsky
Design by Dorothy Lin
Typeset in Self Modern and Neue Haas Grotesk
Printed at Musumeci, Italy

Distributed by SPD / Small Press Distribution
www.spdbooks.org

Published by Wendy's Subway
379 Bushwick Avenue
Brooklyn, NY 11206ca
www.wendyssubway.com

Wendy's Subway is a non-profit reading room, writing space, and independent publisher located in Brooklyn.

The Document Series is an interdisciplinary publishing initiative that highlights work by time-based artists in printed form.

The archival materials in this publication were produced by Jaime Shearn Coan, David Thomson, Mariana Valencia, Tara Aisha Willis, Takahiro Yamamoto, and Mlondi Zondi from June 11–16, 2019 during a Watershed Residency co-curated by Jaime Shearn Coan and Tara Aisha Willis at Mount Tremper Arts. Mount Tremper Arts (MTA) is an artist-founded laboratory space dedicated to supporting artists in the creation and presentation of new works of contemporary art.

Special thanks from the editors to Crystal Wei, Ethan Knechel, Megan Byrne, and the rest of the staff at Mount Tremper Arts. Thanks to Yolanda Royster for lights and sounds. Thanks to Co-founder and Curatorial Director Mathew Pokoik for extending the curatorial invitation and to Program Director Carter Edwards for helping to develop the concept of the residency.

Wendy's Subway would like to thank Simran Ankolkar, Emily Bartsch, and Sebastian Zinn.

This publication is supported, in part, by public funds from the New York City Department of Cultural Affairs in partnership with the City Council.

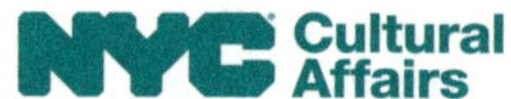

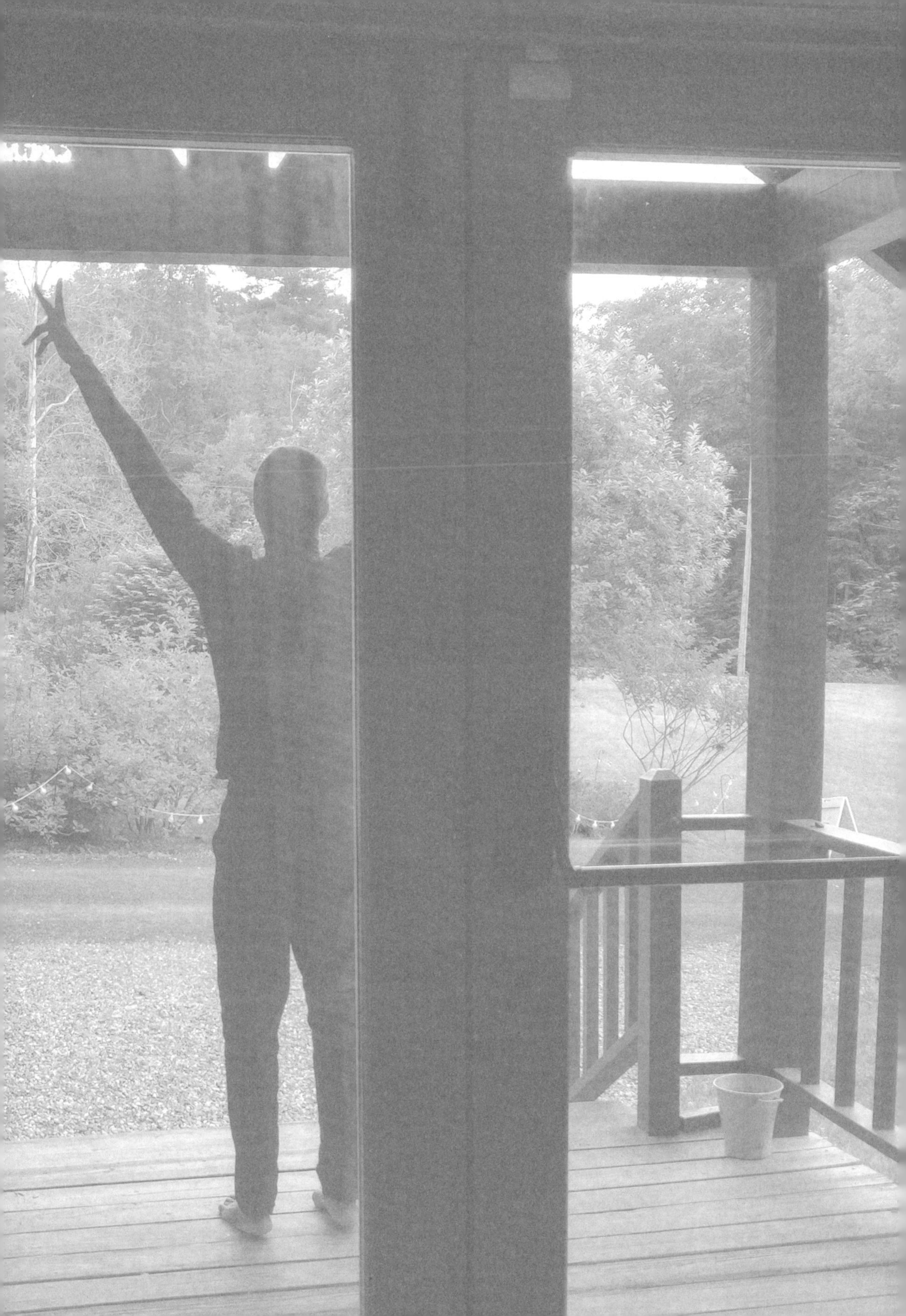

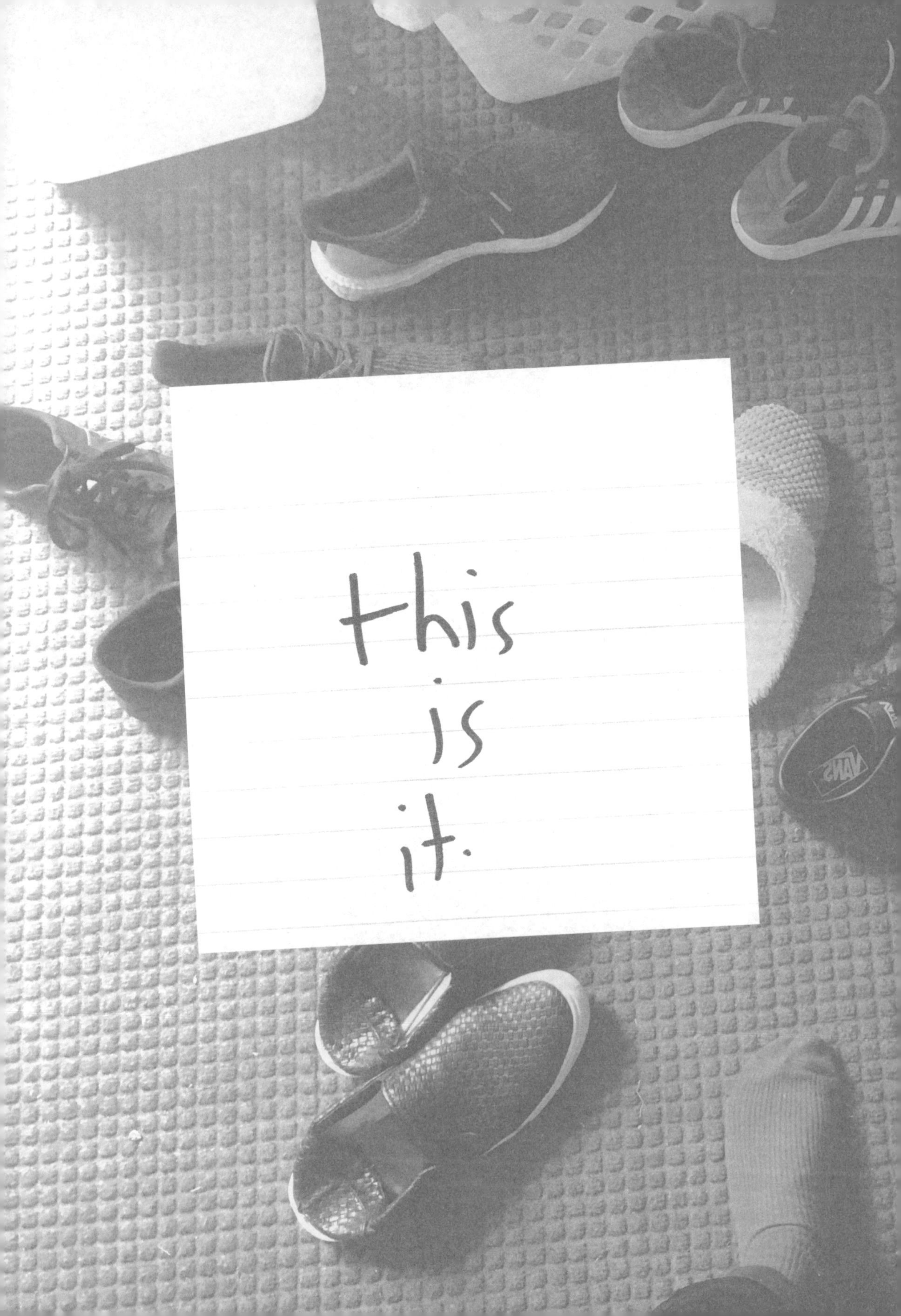
this
is
it.

The moment of encounter: the performance which is the meeting of the reader and the written. What carries through and what transforms within the temporal and spatial limits of the page? The "it" implies a finite, coherent thing. Trailing behind or starting things off (depending on how you see it), "this" narrows it down and makes it vague: this *specific* one (which exactly?). "Is" slips in, conclusively, announcing that doing spells out being. There are the times where it all lines up and you think, *this is it*. It's not *it* exactly but more like the future ghost of something you had forgotten. And a hunger for more arrives. And with that, it's gone. We are supposed to know that first comes before, then now, then after. To write with a beginning, middle, end: each sentence sequential, fractaling toward sense. This seems limited, but there are things in a performance, too, that are about a before or that must precede an after. A conclusion is not the same as an ending. I'm seeking a kind of open sense, sense untied to social codes or individual cognition. If this is it, then that is it, too. If this is an ending, this also leads to an opening. *This is it* is a feeling. A culmination and an interval. As soon as the moment is felt in the body, it's something else altogether. The memory of itself alongside a new now. Here is a stage, here is a studio, here is a door. To disappear through; from which to emerge.

JSC & TAW
JULY 11–12, 2020

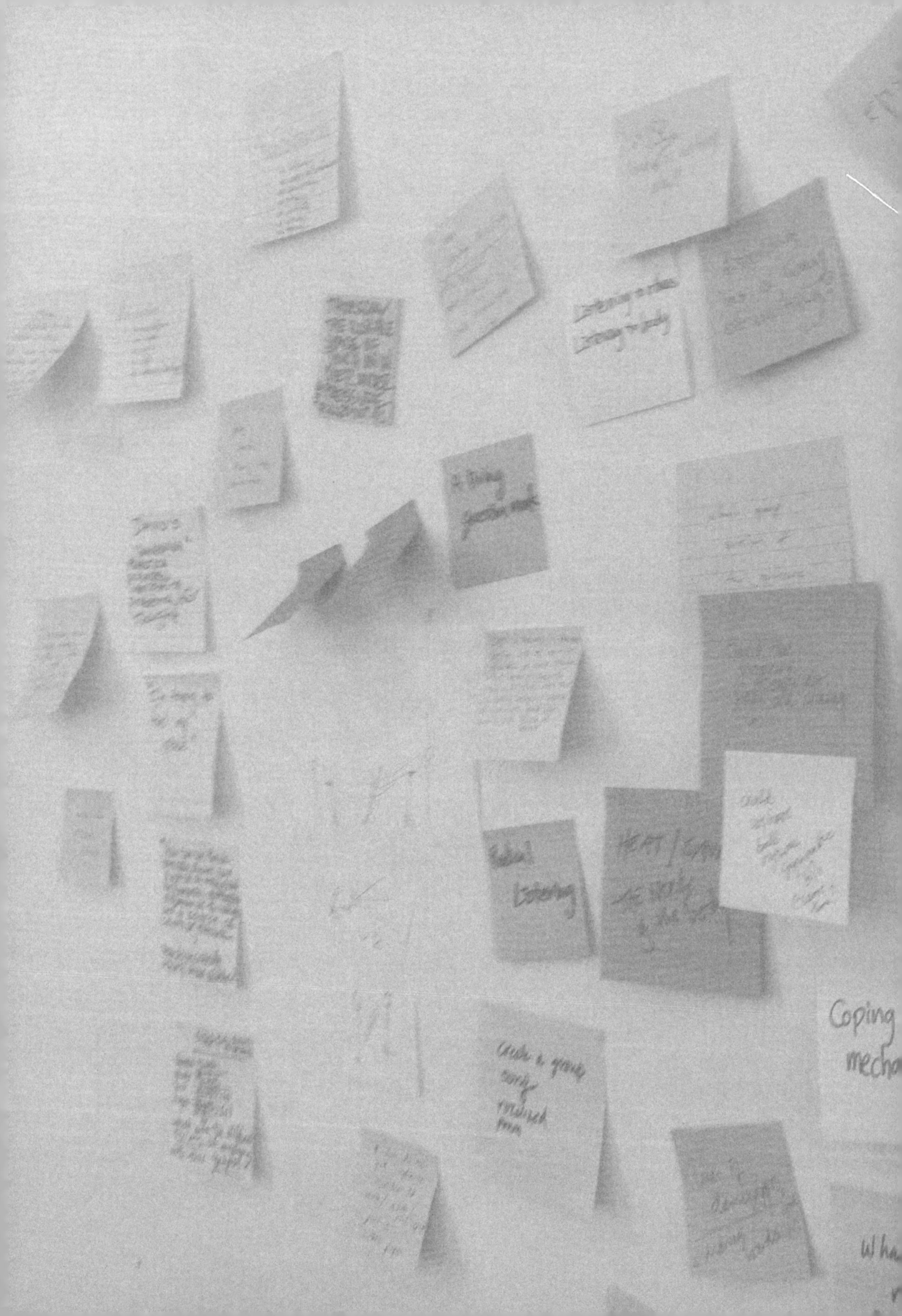
Coping